The Bride Did What?!

The Bride Did What?!

ooooo

Etiquette for the Wedding Impaired

ooooo

Martha A. Woodham

Illustrations by Walter Cumming

LONGSTREET PRESS, INC.
Atlanta, Georgia

Published by
LONGSTREET PRESS, INC.
A subsidiary of Cox Newspapers,
A division of Cox Enterprises, Inc.
2140 Newmarket Parkway, Suite 118
Marietta, GA 30067

Printed in the United States of America
1st printing 1995
Library of Congress Catalog Card Number: 94-74232
ISBN 1-56352-198-9

Book and jacket design by Jill Dible

Printed by Horowitz/Rae, Fairfield, New Jersey

Electronic film prep and separations by Advertising Technologies, Inc., Atlanta, Georgia

Cover: Photograph by Denis Reggie at the Cathedral of Christ the King, Atlanta. Model: Jennifer Johnson, Atlanta. Dress from the Diamond Collection. Flowers by Marvin Gardens Designs, Atlanta.

Photographs courtesy of the *Atlanta Journal and Constitution*, unless otherwise noted.

To my husband, Dr. G. Frank Jenkins, who said
no one would believe that I was an expert on
weddings unless I were married.

Contents

○○○○○

Acknowledgments ◠ ix

Introduction ◠ xi

1. Marriage Myths ◠ 1

2. The Inelegant Bride ◠ 21

3. My Wedding Must Be Perfect Because It's "My Day" ◠ 47

4. "It's My Party" ◠ 77

5. The Tackiest Brides in the World ◠ 115

Acknowledgments

Thanks to my parents, Polly and Willis Woodham, who always told me I could achieve my goal. And extra thanks to my dad for making sure I always had "boy insurance"—a horse—as a teenager. Of course, that's why I didn't get married until I was 39.

I would also like to thank friends who shared their memories of tacky weddings: Anne Barge Clegg, Esther and Mary Civille, Ellen Cruikshank, Matilda Dobbs, Lynn Dupuis, Betsy Eastman, Cindy Fowler, Paige Harvey, Mary Holdt, Paula Hovater, Barbara Jabaley, Rheta Grimsley Johnson, Jennifer McLaurin, Tania McMenamin, Joan O'Harro, Faith Peppers, Robyn Spizman, Meg Reggie, Susan Rountree, Maryln Schwartz, Saye Sutton, Jackie Wammock, Sylvia Weinstock, Betty Jean Weltner, Marlan Wilbanks, and my editor, Suzanne Comer Bell.

And an extra thank-you to wedding photographer Denis Reggie of Atlanta, a bride's best friend.

Introduction

A fast-food chain once told America to "have it your way." Unfortunately, many brides now apply that slogan to their weddings.

These brides want everything "their" way on their day, ignoring tradition, well-meaning mamas, and cautioning friends. They churn out tasteless weddings devoid of the richness of one of life's greatest ceremonies.

Society developed etiquette for a reason. It's a time-tested method designed to get us through life with a minimum of fuss. Manners are the linen napkin on the fast-food counter of American society.

In the South, manners are as important as your family tree. Got a few bad apples hanging on yours? No problem—if you remember to say "please" and "thank you." Manners will always get you by.

By virtue of being so polite, Southerners see themselves as *the* arbiters of good taste. It's part of their heritage, like saying "y'all" and eating grits. Anyone who doesn't have manners is immediately deemed "tacky," as in "Oh, how tacky!" or "Isn't she tacky?"

According to the dictionary, "tacky" describes someone without style or good taste. We Southerners extend that to cover someone who is gaudy and showy, even trashy. Author Maryln Schwartz, who keeps an eye on society in Dallas, says "tacky" includes anyone who puts dark meat in her chicken salad or wears white shoes before Memorial Day.

Who's tacky? Many of those whose faces appear regularly in the tabloids can be classified as truly tacky. Sharon Stone is tacky. Fergie is tacky, but Princess Di isn't. Marla Maples Trump was tacky before she landed the Donald. Loni Anderson and Dolly Parton are tacky but sweet. Madonna is, as we say in the South, too tacky for words.

As etiquette columnist for *Elegant Bride* magazine, I get to say who and what are tacky. My qualifications are impressive: I come from a long line of outspoken Southern women who would rather be dead than tacky.

In fact, my grandmother never recovered from an unexpected visit from our minister. He didn't call first (tacky), and Grandma was mortified when he caught her barefoot (really tacky). My aunt is convinced that's what killed her.

From my years of counseling brides, I've found that couples—and their families—tend to lapse into tackiness as they plan "their day." People are miffed over supposed slights, and the touchy subject of money trips up many a poor bride. When a bride starts referring to "the wedding of my dreams" or "my day," watch out! She's falling into the "Queen for a Day" syndrome, heading straight toward tackiness.

I was inspired, if you can call it that, to write this book to spare brides-to-be from misinformation overload. Everyone has opinions about what's correct at weddings, which they feel compelled to pass along with dire warnings about being improper.

As a South Carolina bride once said, "Weddings are a public expression of your taste." I see *The Bride Did* What?! as my small part in helping the world become a more beautiful, gracious, untacky place.

The Bride Did What?!

1 Marriage Myths

Brides and grooms get so much advice—most of it wrong—that they panic. It's like having a baby: as soon as people find out you're expecting a wedding, they feel free to tell you what to do, along with dire warnings about being improper (i.e. tacky).

Your mother is sure she knows what's correct. His mother has her own ideas, and your neighbor down the street can't wait to tell you horror stories about the tacky weddings she's attended. You begin to feel queasy at the thought of "Your Day."

Well, worry no more. Here are the Top Ten Marriage Myths—and the right answers, no matter what anyone says. Folks will swear these myths are the eternal Etiquette Truth etched in stone and handed down by some great Etiquette God. They aren't, and you can quote me:

Top Ten Marriage Myths

ooooo

10. THE BRIDE AND GROOM MUST ASK THEIR SIBLINGS TO BE BRIDESMAIDS AND GROOMSMEN.

Although it is customary to ask brothers and sisters to be attendants, the bride and groom are free to ask whomever they wish— best friends, pals from the office, a buddy from a favorite bar.

But this could be deadly. Friends come and go, while your families are there forever. You avoid a lot of hurt feelings by asking brothers and sisters.

Tacky brides wail, "But I don't feel *close* to his sisters. I want my friends instead." A wedding is a great place to get acquainted. After the "I do's," those strangers will be *your* sisters, too.

9. THE BRIDE MUST BE ESCORTED DOWN THE AISLE AND GIVEN AWAY BY SOMEONE.

Being given away is a tradition that evolved from the days when men bought brides from their fathers or, even worse, captured them.

Today many young women feel this custom is archaic. Somehow it was charming when a woman went from her father's home directly to her new husband's, but that's not true of most couples today. With so many women going to college, supporting themselves, and marrying later, being "given away" seems terribly out of date. If you don't want it, leave it out. Ask your minister to delete it from the service.

And, if you choose, you *can* walk down the aisle by yourself. Not every bride has a father; not every bride *likes* her father. Some brides say going solo made them feel like royalty.

8. THE BRIDE'S FATHER MUST SIT IN THE FIRST PEW WITH THE BRIDE'S MOTHER, EVEN IF THEY HATE THE SIGHT OF EACH OTHER.

In a perfect world, divorced mothers and fathers would overcome their loathing so all could be sweetness and light on their child's wedding day.

Let's get real. Divorce is a nineties fact of life. When divorced parents get along, it's wonderful. Mom and Dad can sit together, one big happy parental unit on the first pew.

This changes if stepparents are in the picture. Mom—and her new husband—should sit in the first pew. Dad—and his new wife—should sit in the next pew. If they do not get along, Dad and his new wife should sit even farther back in the church—far enough away to avoid bodily harm. (All of this goes for the groom's parents, too.)

By the way, any former stepparents would be treated as guests.

7. THE NUMBER OF GROOMSMEN MUST EQUAL THE NUMBER OF BRIDESMAIDS.

So who's counting? Unlike many other areas of modern life, there is no rule that says a wedding party must have equality. An equal number of men and women makes a pretty picture at the altar—and makes life easier for the wedding consultant—but this is not mandatory. You can have all men, all women—even all children if you like. You don't have to be politically correct at your wedding.

6. A Bride Cannot Ask Her Mother to Be Matron of Honor.

> *"If you obey all the rules, you miss all the fun."*
>
> — Katharine Hepburn, actress

If a father can be a best man, there is no reason a mother can't be matron of honor. It's a beautiful, loving gesture.

The only drawback is if the wedding is a very large one. The mother of the bride and the matron of honor each may have so many duties that it might be a burden to ask your mom to undertake both jobs. But if your mom is extremely organized and is your best friend, ask her.

6a. A Bride Cannot Ask Her Mother to Escort Her Down the Aisle.

If a father can escort his daughter, there is no reason . . . see No. 6 above.

More and more brides are asking their moms to make the stroll down the aisle instead of benchwarming the first pew. This custom is borrowed from Jewish ceremonies, where both parents escort the bride and groom.

It is a lovely gesture, and most moms are thrilled to be asked.

5. A Flower Girl Must Be under Age Six.

The littler they are, the cuter they are—and the more they can disrupt your ceremony! The same goes for ring bearers.

Flower girls have refused to go down the aisle or toss their petals. One little ring bearer grabbed the flower girl's basket, dumped the petals in a pile, and began jumping on it. And my mom loves to tell of when I was a flower girl: at a crucial moment in the ceremony, I stage-whispered, "Mommy, I have to tee-tee."

The only criterion for the job of flower girl or ring bearer should be how important a child is to you. If the little girl or little boy is someone you want to include, by all means do it, no matter how old—or young—the child is.

4. Brides and Grooms Must Pick Attendants Who Are Close to Their Own Age.

No, the only requirement for being an attendant is a sincere attachment to the bride or groom—and the ability to pay for the clothing.

I know of brides in their twenties who had bridesmaids in their sixties, and the weddings were full of love and rejoicing.

3. A Pregnant Woman Cannot Be a Bridesmaid.

It is a mystery to me why it is considered poor manners to have a pregnant woman participate in a ceremony so full of fertility symbols.

Traditionally, bridesmaids were young women who surrounded the bride to confuse any evil spirits lurking about. Perhaps a bridesmaid had to be fleet-footed, and it's hard to run when you are pregnant.

I see no problems with asking a friend who is with child, other than logistical ones: she may have trouble fitting into her dress.

Being practical, I realize that a very pregnant bridesmaid may cause a stir. If she is toward the end of her term, she may also be uncomfortable standing for long periods of time. (She should also allow for an unexpected early delivery.) You should give her the option of gracefully bowing out, solicitously stressing her comfort, of course. Do *not* tell her she looks like a cow.

2. "An Overweight Bridesmaid Will Ruin My Wedding."

What is this, a beauty contest? Friendship is not just skin deep. If you care enough about someone to be her friend, her looks shouldn't matter just because you are getting married.

Again, be practical. People will talk about someone who is distressingly overweight. The bridesmaid's comfort and ease should be your primary considerations.

1. "I Can Only Have One Maid of Honor and One Matron of Honor."

You may have two of either if you wish. Simply call them "honor attendants" and divide their duties.

And don't limit yourself to women. If your best friend is a guy, ask him. Just don't call him, as one Atlanta bride did, your "mister of honor."

The Top Wedding Myth of All Time

ooooo

THE BRIDE'S FAMILY HAS TO FOOT ALL OF THE WEDDING BILLS.

A cartoon strip shows a character pondering "another of life's great mysteries." "If women are equal to men," he asks, "why do the bride's parents have to pay for the wedding?"

Once upon a time, the bride's father had that dubious honor, but life is no longer a fairy tale. Weddings are so expen-

sive that often the groom's family offers to share the costs.

The operative word is "offers." One commandment in the Etiquette Bible is: There shalt be no dunning of the groom's parents.

TACKY PENALTIES

Etiquette allows you a grace period, but after that, tacky penalties accrue:

◆ You should answer invitations the next day.

◆ You have two weeks to write a thank-you note.

◆ You have a year to send a wedding gift.

> *"Manners are the happy way of doing things."*
>
> —Ralph Waldo Emerson, American essayist

They may offer to pay for the flowers, for instance, or for the liquor, but you can't force them. It's tacky.

Older couples who marry—if you call the thirties and onward old—often decide to pay for everything themselves. They usually are financially established, and by paying for the wedding, they can be sure it will be exactly to their tastes.

A bride marrying for the second—or even the third time—should not expect her parents to foot the bill again. They have done their parental duty, and she should not expect more. It's tacky.

Dress Do's and Don'ts

ooooo

Part of the fun of a wedding is that everyone gets to dress up and look fabulous. Part of the headache of a wedding is getting the clothes right.

Weddings are probably the most formal occasions many of us will ever attend. No one wants to be overdressed or—horrors!—underdressed. A guy gets grumpy if he mistakenly shows up in a dark suit when everyone else is in tuxedos.

Let's get these common misconceptions out of the closet and pin down the right information:

WRONG! Only a Virgin Can Wear a White Wedding Dress.

RIGHT! In the days when men bought brides, it was very important for a woman to be a virgin when she married. After all, the groom didn't want used merchandise.

During the Victorian era, the white wedding gown came to symbolize virginity, and this tradition endures today—whether the bride is a virgin or not.

Today's first-time bride has a lot of options — candlelight or ivory gowns, pale pastels—as well as white. The woman who is marrying for the second—or even third—time should remember the titter factor. If she doesn't want any snickering from the crowd, she should

---

HOW TO TELL A TACKY BRIDE

◆ Her beaded headpiece comes down in a vee on her forehead.

◆ A tulle pouf sticks up in the back like a rooster tail.

◆ She wears fake nails with rhinestones.

---

select colors other than white.

The difference here is how many times a woman has been married, *not* whether she's a virgin.

WRONG! Mothers of the Bride and Groom Must Wear Dresses That Match the Wedding Party.

REALLY BAD IDEAS

- ◈ Electric blue lace Madonna gloves for the bridesmaids

- ◈ Bridesmaids in different pastel shades

- ◈ Bridesmaids in hoopskirts carrying parasols

- ◈ Mothers of the bride (or groom) in sequins during a daytime wedding

- ◈ Big hair

- ◈ Blue tuxes

- ◈ Cummerbunds to match the bridesmaids' dresses

- ◈ White leather wedding dresses

RIGHT! Officially, the mothers aren't part of the wedding party, so their attire need not be in the same color scheme as the bridesmaids' gowns.

But their gowns should match the degree of formality of the wedding. For example, at an informal daytime wedding, the mothers should wear street-length dresses or suits. For an ultra-formal evening wedding, their gowns should be elegant and full-length.

The mothers coordinate their outfits so they complement each other in degree of formality. You don't want one mother in a long gown and the other in something she'd wear to the office.

Tradition has it that the mother of the bride makes her selection first, and the mother of the groom follows her cue. But if the groom's mother jumps the gun and chooses her gown first, don't worry about it. Fretting over frocks is silly.

WRONG! Mothers of the Bride and Groom Cannot Wear Dresses That Are the Same Color.

RIGHT! Sure they can. They should wear what looks best on them. If both of them think blue is "their" color, then they both should feel free to wear it. However, they may prefer to choose different shades of blue—so they won't end up looking like twins.

WRONG! Bridesmaids Can Never Wear Black.

RIGHT! Once true, but no longer. Designers are coming out with exciting gowns in black for bridesmaids. The more conservative dresses pair colorful tops with black skirts, and others have colorful accents.

A word of caution: Black is a powerful fashion statement and looks best at more formal evening weddings.

"*You can get through life with bad manners, but it's easier with good manners.*"

—Lillian Gish, American actress

Raleigh, N.C., residents are still laughing over the wedding where the bridesmaids wore all black — and so did the bride!

RULES NEVER TO BREAK

◈ Always say please and thank you.

◈ The bride's mother, sisters, or aunts cannot host a shower.

◈ Always write your thank-you notes promptly.

◈ Always be gracious.

WRONG! BRIDESMAIDS MUST WEAR PASTELS IN THE SUMMER. DARK COLORS ARE WORN ONLY IN THE FALL OR WINTER.
RIGHT! This is another fashion law that's been overruled. Brides are picking their favorites, no matter what time of year. The trick is to keep the fabrics seasonal. Velvet, for instance, just isn't the thing for a summer wedding, and cotton won't do for a formal winter wedding.

A bride should also consider what's appropriate in prints. Dark plaids are more wintery than flowery pastels. If you are still in doubt, ask your wedding shop consultant.

WRONG! A WOMAN IS NOT REALLY ENGAGED UNTIL SHE WEARS A DIAMOND ENGAGEMENT RING.
RIGHT! Engagement rings are a nicety, not a necessity. While a ring can be a shining token of a man's pledge to a woman, that pledge need not be symbolized by precious metals or gems.

Some couples prefer to wear similar gold wedding bands and no other adornments. Some prefer other stones, such as a beloved birthstone or a mix of diamonds and colored stones. Still others may opt for an antique ring as a wedding ring without a band. It's the couple's decision.

WRONG! GUESTS CANNOT WEAR BLACK OR WHITE TO A WEDDING.
RIGHT! At one time, white and black were indeed taboo for guests. The reasoning was, a guest in white looked as if she were trying to show up the bride. Black, the color of mourning, was considered bad luck.

These traditions have changed, and black is acceptable even for bridesmaids' dresses. One bride's three sisters all wore black, in mourning, they joked, for the poor guy who was marrying their sibling.

Some brides even have all-white weddings, but when it comes to guest attire, white is still primarily reserved for the bride.

WRONG! MY FIANCÉ IS IN THE MILITARY SERVICE, BUT HE DOESN'T HAVE TO WEAR HIS DRESS UNIFORM.
RIGHT! His dress blues, as they are called, are considered the military equivalent of civilian formalwear, so, yes, he must wear that uniform. The same holds true for any male mem-

"Tact consists in knowing how far to go too far."

—Jean Cocteau, French man of letters

"*When two people are under the influence of the most violent, most insane, most delusive and most transient of passions, they are required to swear that they will remain in that excited, abnormal and exhausting condition continuously until death do them part.*"

—George Bernard Shaw, Irish playwright

bers of the wedding party who are in the military.

But no dowdy uniform, please, for a bride who is in the service. She may wear the traditional bridal gown. Any bridesmaids who are in the service also may wear gowns instead of their uniforms.

Here's a tip: A boutonniere is not worn with a military uniform.

WRONG! For a Formal Wedding, Brides Should Put "Black Tie Invited" or "Black Tie Preferred" on the Wedding Invitations.
RIGHT! Here is a tacky trend that needs to be put out of its misery before it can spread. This lame attempt at etiquette by bride magazines creates a situation that satisfies no one. It sounds as if you are inviting a suit!

Guests should *know* to wear black tie for

formal or ultraformal weddings held after 6:00 p.m. If you want to be sure, have "Black Tie" printed in the lower right-hand corner of the invitation. Don't be wishy-washy about it.

LETTER FROM A REAL BRIDE: I would like my formal daytime wedding to be a black-tie affair. I really want my guests to dress in formal attire because I believe the photos will look more like a wedding and less like a gathering of friends. Is black tie restricted to formal evening weddings or can I really have my daytime wedding a black-tie affair?. . .   — LOVES THE LOOK

DEAR LOVES: Don't look to me for permission to violate the "no black tie before 6:00 p.m." rule. Not only would it be incredibly tacky, you would confuse your wedding guests, who know perfectly well that a tuxedo is not worn in the daytime. It's one thing if you want to be gauche, but it's not fair to your guests, whose attire should not be dictated by unsophisticated brides. If you want everyone in black tie, change the time of your wedding.

RULES TO BREAK

💎 Your bridesmaids can't wear black.

💎 You have to put tissue in your invitations.

💎 Your mother can't escort you down the aisle.

💎 The groom has to have male attendants, and the bride has to have female.

WRONG! "I Want My Groom to Stand Out at the Wedding, so I Want Him to Wear a Red Bow Tie and Cummerbund while the Groomsmen Wear Black."
RIGHT! Why? Are you afraid you won't recognize him? The men in the wedding party should all dress alike, particularly if they are wearing tuxedos. The only time variation is allowed is for daytime weddings. If the attire is gray cutaways or strollers, the groom and the best man dress alike. The ushers and the fathers may have subtle variations in the gray tone of the trousers and the stripe of their ascots.

WRONG! Guests Who Are Not Members of the Wedding Party Cannot Wear Dresses the Color of the Bridesmaids' Gowns.
RIGHT! How is a guest going to know the color of the gowns until the bridesmaids make their entrance? If you are a guest at a wedding, wear what is appropriate and don't worry about looking as if you are going to crash the wedding party.

WRONG! It Is Now Considered Correct for a Woman Who Has Been Married to Wear a White Dress, Particularly if She Had

> "My boyfriend and I broke up. He wanted to get married, and I didn't want him to."
>
> —Rita Rudner, American comedian

A SMALL WEDDING OR ELOPED THE FIRST TIME. RIGHT! Just because a woman did not get to play bride in a beautiful white gown the first time she married is no reason for her to trot out all the finery the second time around. A white gown with a long train and veil is reserved for the young and inexperienced bride.

A second-time bride should wear a simple dress that complements her simple ceremony. Although a suit is better, a long gown is acceptable, but it should be pastel or have pastel accents. It should not be as ornate as a wedding gown. She should not wear a veil.

FAMOUS LAST WORDS FROM THE BRIDE TO THE BRIDESMAIDS

"You'll be able to wear this again."

According to the Guinness Book of Records, the world's longest wedding dress train was just over 97 feet, 7 inches, and was worn by a British bride in 1990.

BRIDAL STRIP TEASE

Planning to wear elbow-length gloves? There's no way you can remove them gracefully without looking like Gypsy Rose Lee. Instead, open the seam.

TOO TACKY FOR WORDS

Brides who change clothes several times during the reception. As the evening goes on, each dress gets shorter—and skimpier!

WILL THE REAL BRIDE PLEASE STAND UP?

A Connecticut bride became engaged to a cross dresser, and they both wanted to wear long white gowns and veils. Another bride, this one from New York, thought it would be a great joke on her wedding guests if she and her fiancé both wore wedding gowns.

HEADS, YOU LOSE

A bride with a sixpence in her shoe for luck found that it brought her pain instead. Halfway down the aisle, she halted, hiked up her skirts, took the coin out of her shoe and threw it away.

THE ULTIMATE "SOMETHING BORROWED"

When Marla Maples married New York developer Donald Trump, she wore a borrowed diamond tiara worth $2 million.

ON THREE: I DO-BE-DO-BE-DO

A bride planning her church wedding wanted the groom and his attendants to wear top hats and carry canes. Only, said the groom, if they could break into "New York, New York" at the altar.

> *"Marriage is a great institution, if you like living in an institution."*
>
> —Mae West, American actress

*Wedding consultants have
a special name for brides
who are difficult and obnoxious:*

BRIDEZILLA.

2
The Inelegant Bride

The Worst Etiquette Blunders

ooooo

Weddings are not only times of great joy and rejoicing, but they are also prime opportunities for tremendous social blunders. Perhaps the worst faux pas are committed by tittering guests looking for imagined errors, but here are some real mistakes for everyone to avoid:

THE BRIDE WHO PUTS HERSELF FIRST

♥ Nothing is as unlovely as a petulant bride who wants her way on "her day." The gracious bride who puts others first is a true etiquette queen.

FORCING RELATIVES TO PAY FOR THE "WEDDING OF MY DREAMS"

♥ Many couples dream of weddings too grand for their parents' pocketbooks. They should accept their parents' budget restrictions and scale back their plans with grace and good humor—or pay for everything themselves.

PRETENDING YOUR PARENTS ARE NOT DIVORCED

♥ Everyone was aghast when a bride took the microphone at her reception to ask her divorced parents to dance together "once again, just for me, on my special day."

Weddings are family time. Unfortunately, not all families today fit the Norman Rockwell image of perfection, so don't try to create an instant happy family for the wedding-day photos. Instead, seat parents who don't get along in separate pews and at separate tables. Shoot photos with both sets of parents and stepparents. Have corsages and boutonnieres for everyone.

COUPLES WHO TELL THEIR GUESTS WHAT TO GIVE THEM

♥ No matter how nicely it's done, there is no polite way to dictate what guests give you. The reason? When you tell someone what to give you, it no longer is freely given and becomes social blackmail.

So do not mention gifts on your wedding invitations and do NOT include a list of stores where you are registered with the invitation (believe it or not, this has been done).

It's also considered extremely tacky to ask guests to donate to your new mortgage or your honeymoon. As manners maven Letitia Baldrige drolly says, "Wedding presents should be items the couple fights over if there's a divorce."

COUPLES WHO TELL THEIR GUESTS WHAT NOT TO GIVE THEM

♥ Even if you have been living together for ten years and have every kitchen gadget in the Williams-Sonoma catalog, do not tell your guests you don't want any gifts. This also applies to well-meaning couples who request a donation to their favorite charity. The reasoning is the same: friends and family who want to surprise and thrill you resent being told how to spend their money.

THANK-YOU NOTES THAT ARE LATE OR — GASP! — NEVER WRITTEN

This is the biggest complaint about brides and grooms. Not thanking someone for a gift (or a party) is appalling conduct, and it is inexcusable. The rules are:

◆ An oral thanks is not enough.

◆ You have two weeks to write the note on nice paper with no mistakes.

(By the way, unless his hand is broken, the groom should also participate.)

"The gentle mind by gentle deeds is known, / For a man by nothing is so well betrayed as by his manners."

—Edmund Spenser, English poet

"I couldn't believe it when I got a thank-you note from my cousin," says an Arizona woman. "Her notes were printed, 'Thank you for coming to our wedding. We appreciate the _____.' And she had filled in the blank!"

WEDDING PROGRAMS THAT DETAIL THE LIVES OF THE WEDDING PARTY

💜 Some brides go overboard with the information in their wedding programs. Guests learn that bridesmaid No. 1, Shirley, loves to ski, while groomsman No. 4, John, is a newlywed himself. How cute.

A wedding program is not a playbill, with biographies of all the actors. If you must have a program, give just the basics, please.

STALLING GUESTS AT THE RECEPTION WHILE PHOTOGRAPHS ARE BEING TAKEN

💜 It's not polite to keep your guests waiting, so keep photos to a minimum after the ceremony. Do plan for guests to be served drinks and hors d'oeuvres until the wedding party arrives.

Unfortunately, some couples are scheduling their receptions two to four hours after the ceremony is over. This is a bad idea: It's hard on everyone involved, particularly out-of-town guests who find themselves all dressed up with time to kill. You can't exactly hang out in the mall in a sequined gown.

GARTER GUIDELINE

💜 Don't let the groom go for the garter with his teeth. And watch where you place the garter. Below the knee is much more discreet.

"BLACK TIE INVITED"

💜 This meaningless phrase has come into vogue with wedding consultants, but it simply confuses your guests. It sounds as if you are inviting a suit of clothes.

The dress code for your wedding is dictated by the time of the ceremony coupled with the formality of the bridal gown. Male guests should wear dark suits to most weddings, but most evening weddings call for black tie or the ultraformal white tie. If you think guests need a hint, put "Black Tie" or "White Tie" in the lower left-hand corner of the reception invitation, never on the ceremony invitation.

WEARING A VEIL AS A SECOND-TIME BRIDE

♥ Every bride deserves a fabulous gown, but only a first-time bride is entitled to wear a veil with her finery. This ancient tradition has to do with the innocence of the bride. It looks silly for a woman who has been married and has four kids to pretend that dewy-eyed innocence.

SIGNS THE BRIDE MAY BE TOO YOUNG TO GET MARRIED

◆ She can't vote yet.

◆ Her invitations are decorated with the Precious Moments bride and groom.

◆ Her wedding has a pink teddy bear theme.

When a bridesmaid canceled just two days before the wedding (tacky), an Atlanta bride called another friend to ask her to fill in (really tacky). The substitute refused. "I wasn't about to be a B-list bridesmaid," she said. "Besides, the bride wanted me just so she wouldn't have to pay for the dress."

REMEMBERING A DECEASED PARENT

Many couples want to honor their deceased parents in some way during their wedding. They may light a candle in his or her memory, or lay a bouquet of flowers in the front pew.

These are lovely thoughts, but such public displays are sadly out of place at a wedding. A wedding is a time of joy and rejoicing, and death should not be allowed to intrude.

If there is to be any memorial, it should be done privately. I prefer to see the bride wear her late mother's jewelry or the groom carry his father's watch. These gestures truly come from the heart.

"We're having a little disagreement. What I want is a big church wedding with bridesmaids and flowers and a no-expense-spared reception, and what he wants is to break off our engagement."

—Sally Poplin

As the minister presented the married couple to a church full of guests at a very formal wedding, the bride couldn't restrain herself. "Yes!" she shouted, pumping her arm in victory.

CHARITY BEGINS AT HOME

. . . And so do manners. Unfortunately, some people are more polite to banktellers and sales clerks than to their own kin.

The stress of a wedding can magnify this, sometimes creating rifts in families that aren't easily mended. No amount of pure white tulle and sweet bridal cake can heal those wounds.

The gracious bride finds that a smiling "thank you" can ease the strains and a diplomatic "I'll think about it" will avoid hurt feelings. She knows that people are more apt to do as she asks if a "please" is attached, and she never forgets to let her parents know how much she appreciates their sacrifices for her happiness.

The gracious bride knows that courtesy and kindness don't end when she takes off her veil. Courtesy is the most important furnishing in her new home.

UH OH

💜 Good Advice: It's better emotionally and financially to back out before you say "I do" than after—even if you have to send all the gifts back.

💜 "I knew I had made a mistake by the time we got to the back of the church," says one recent divorcée.

💜 Hundreds of guests came to Atlanta for a weekend of wedding festivities. The bride and groom organized golf and tennis tournaments, shopping trips, and brunches. Finally, everyone gathered at the Ritz-Carlton Buckhead for the wedding, but there was no bride or groom. The minutes passed, and the rabbi came into the room. The wedding was off, he told the astonished crowd, but the couple wanted everyone to enjoy the reception anyway. Eventually the couple joined their guests for the party. Later, they took what would have been their honeymoon together. After all, it was paid for!

"Weddings are an expression of your taste," said a South Carolina bride. The first thing she did after becoming engaged was to join the most exclusive Episcopal church in town.

SCANDALOUS V. TACKY

Never mistake the Scandalous Bride for a Tacky Bride. The Scandalous Bride truly knows how to shock friends and family. In some parts of the country, obvious pregnancy is no longer taboo enough to put a bride into the scandalous category. She would have to do something worse, like marry her sister's husband after a torrid affair.

Scarlett of *Gone With the Wind* fame would have been a Scandalous Bride when she stole her sister's fiancé, but no one noticed except poor Sue Ellen. You will see more Scandalous Brides on TV than in real life, but they are out there.

THESE ARE TACKY BRIDES

♥ The bride who had her ex-husband give her away

♥ The bride who invited her newly discovered birthparents to the wedding without informing her adoptive parents. "I wanted it to be a surprise," she said.

♥ The bride who married for the third time, in white, to a man younger than her son and she was the town's wedding consultant.

♥ The bride who wrote a long poem to the groom and had it read during the wedding by her teenaged brother. Guests struggled to stifle their laughter as the boy read, "When I met you I was only a child, but now I am a woman."

❈ ❈ ❈ ❈ ❈ ❈ ❈ ❈ ❈

One nervous Richmond bride lost her cookies at the altar. A friend sent her a card: "Congratulations, Fountain-Face!"

❈ ❈ ❈ ❈ ❈ ❈ ❈ ❈ ❈

PUBLICITY

Of course you want to tell the world about your wedding, but a huge full-length photo in the nation's newspapers is overdoing it. Here are some guidelines:

◈ More and more newspapers are charging for wedding write-ups and photos. Trying to have the largest photo in the *New York Times* is gauche.

◈ Don't describe your dress in your story. No one knows what Alençon lace is, anyway.

◈ Don't send a professional press kit to magazines like *Town & Country*. A photo and simple write-up are fine.

◈ Do include any pertinent information about your backgrounds, i.e., your grandfather founded Exxon.

After reading the newspaper article describing the "princess bodice" of the bride's gown, my aunt looked at the accompanying photo. "Looks like queen-size to me," she said.

"THE NEKKID PARTY"

While attending her male cousin's wedding reception, a Georgia woman was invited to join the bride and groom later, at a party on a yacht. But when she went up on deck, she was shocked to find the bride and the bridesmaids completely naked. They were all strippers at an Atlanta nightclub. When the story got out in her family, as of course it would, her grandmother kept saying, "I cannot believe I went to the wedding of a stripper." Everyone in the family always referred to that evening as "The Nekkid Party."

> *"I have a view that one should not make the decision to marry unless it is absolutely irresistible."*
>
> —Hilary Rubinstein, English literary agent married for thirty-five years

A young couple came into the county registrar's office. "We need to get a marriage license," the man said, "and I need a gun permit."

She's Gotta Have It: Why Brides Want Big Weddings

ooooo

THE FIRST-TIME BRIDE

♥ My parents will pay for it.

♥ I'll get gobs of presents.

♥ I get to choose whatever I want, and people will actually buy it for me.

♥ It's a huge party for all my friends.

♥ I can have twelve bridesmaids so it looks like I have lots of friends.

♥ I'll be the center of attention for months.

THE SECOND-TIME BRIDE

◈ The first time didn't count.

◈ I didn't get to have the wedding of my dreams the first time.

◈ My ex-husband got all the china.

◈ It's a huge party for all my friends, whom I didn't know the first time I got married.

◈ I'll be the center of attention again.

◈ I want to wear a long white gown because my heart is pure.

◈ This will be my first wedding with the right man.

◈ I can do what I want because it's "my day" (I'm entitled to more than one special day).

◈ Everyone will have to tell me how beautiful I am.

◈ I deserve it.

💜 I didn't get to make my debut.

💜 I can do what I want because it's "my day."

💜 Everyone will have to tell me how beautiful I am.

💜 I deserve it.

IT'S JUST NOT DONE

💜 Posing for your engagement photo in T-shirts with sayings on them

💜 A serenade by the groom during the ceremony

💜 Enclosing your bridal registry list in shower invitations

💜 Asking guests to contribute toward (a) your mortgage, (b) your honeymoon, or (c) your wedding expenses

💜 Displaying gifts at the reception

💜 Asking guests to wear black tie to a day time wedding

♥ Specifying "Adults only" on the reception invitations

♥ Getting engaged before your divorce (or his!) is final

"The Honour of Your Presence"

ooooo

Wording the wedding invitations seems to give brides lots of trouble, and no wonder: today's brides and grooms seem to have at least two sets of parents, and they all want their names on the invitations. Etiquette mavens Amy Vanderbilt and Emily Post never had to face these nineties kinds of problems. "We received a wedding invitation that actually was a computer printout," says one woman. "It was horrible."

THE CLASSIC WEDDING INVITATION

It is traditional for wedding invitations to be issued by the bride's parents, who are *sponsoring* the wedding, not necessarily paying for it. This is how they should look:

Mr. and Mrs. Hugh Ashford Dunwoody
request the honour of your presence
at the marriage of their daughter
Elizabeth Ansley
to
Mr. David William Chastain III
(on) Saturday, the seventh of January
(One thousand nine hundred and ninety-six)
at six o'clock
The Cathedral of Saint Philip
Atlanta

(Words in parentheses are optional).

A separate reception card can be enclosed:

Reception
immediately following the ceremony
The Georgia Club
Atlanta

A combination wedding and reception invitation would say:

Mr. and Mrs. Hugh Ashford Dunwoody
request the honour of your presence
at the marriage of their daughter
Elizabeth Ansley
to
Mr. David William Chastain III
(on) Saturday, the seventh of January
(One thousand nine hundred and ninety-six)
at six o'clock
The Cathedral of Saint Philip
and afterward at
The Georgia Club
Atlanta

Although it is not required, you may add your fiancé's parents if you wish. Their names would go below his.

WHO GETS TOP BILLING?

Wedding invitations should not be a scorecard to indicate who pays for what and how much. This was never a problem until divorce lost its social stigma. In the past, it was considered poor taste for both names of divorced parents to appear on the invitation, but no one seems to care now.

And these days, the groom's parents want to be named, too. You can only hope that they're still married to each other.

To avoid an invitation that would look like a telephone book, list only your natural parents, like this:

Susan Broward Hamilton
and
Roger Gadsden Madison
request the honour of your presence
at the marriage of their daughter
Susan Louise Madison
to
John Thomas Collier
etc. . . .

To add your fiancé's parents, put their names below his or below your parents'. (If the invitation looks cramped, ask your printer about using smaller type.)

If your parents do not get along, consider the old-fashioned route: Your mother issues invitations to the wedding ceremony; your father, to the reception. If they have remarried, include their spouses' names.

If the bride's mother has remarried, she and her new husband would issue the invitation. The wording would be:

Mr. and Mrs. Gerald Franklin Collier
request the honour of your presence
at the marriage of her daughter
Elizabeth Ansley Dunwoody (Note: Use your last name)
etc. . . .

The father—and his wife, if he has remarried—would issue the invitations to the reception. The invitations should be mailed separately.

> "Life is short, but there is always time for courtesy."
>
> —Ralph Waldo Emerson, American essayist

WHAT'S NEXT, TAKING ADVERTISING?

One couple wanted to make sure the backers of their wedding festivities were properly recognized. They listed the people who were paying for the wedding as "Primary Sponsors" and "Secondary Sponsors" on the invitations.

SHE'S GETTING MARRIED AT LAST

Etiquette books never define what they call "the mature bride." We're never told exactly how mature (translation: how old!) she is. But I would put her over thirty and no longer living at home. Anyone who can manage her career and/or children is someone who can issue her own invitations:

The honour of your presence
is requested at the marriage of
Ms. Elizabeth Ansley Dunwoody
to
Mr. David William Chastain III
(on) Saturday, the seventh of January
at six o'clock (in the evening)
The St. Luke's Episcopal Church
Atlanta

(Words in parentheses are optional.)

TOO TACKY FOR WORDS

◈ Saying "Adults-Only Reception"

◈ Response cards that say "Number of guests _____"

◈ The worst: Including the stores where you are registered in your invitations

REPONDEZ, S'IL VOUS PLAÎT

"RSVP" goes in the lower left-hand corner of the reception card. An RSVP is not needed for the church ceremony, but you will need to know how many people are coming to your reception.

Unfortunately that does not mean people will actually respond.

"RSVP" may also be written as follows: "The favor of a reply is requested." Or "Please reply to" and then give an address.

One mother of the bride insisted that guests would not answer wedding invitations if they had to write a response. She printed her phone number on the invitations!

OUT OF THE MOUTH OF BABES

One couple, who had lived together for two years and had a 6-month-old baby, thought it would be clever to include their son in the wedding festivities. Their invitation read:

John Jacob Rogers, Jr.
requests the honour of your presence
at the marriage of
his mother, Janice Ann Woods
to
his father, John Jacob Rogers, Sr.
etc. . . .

The bride said she thought the invitations were "sweetly personal." Wrong! They were Terribly Tacky.

INVITATIONS FROM BEYOND THE GRAVE

Many couples wish to honor a deceased parent by including his or her name on the wedding invitation. It's a sweet thought, but weddings are a time of celebration and joy. There should be no reminders of death.

On a more practical level, a wedding invitation is just that, an invitation. To be blunt, dead people cannot issue invitations. They cannot be hosts. Don't do it.

Do, however, include the names of deceased parents in newspaper announcements. The deceased should be identified as "the late . . ."

One couple couldn't bear the thought of not including their dear departed parents on the wedding invitations. Guests were issued invitations from beyond the grave:

Mrs. Linda Malone and Mr. Robert Fry
and
Mr. William Malone and Mrs. Angela Fry
in spirit
request the honour of your presence
etc. . . .

THE GANG FROM THE OFFICE

If you want to invite your office pals, remember:

◈ You have to include spouses and live-ins.

◈ Mail their invitations to their homes. Tacky people stick the invitation on the bulletin board.

◈ You don't have to invite everyone.

YOU ARE SENDING ME AN INVITATION, AREN'T YOU?

How does the Gracious Bride deal with tacky people who invite themselves to her wedding? She is prepared. She doesn't panic and stammer out something idiotic. She doesn't give in to this rudeness.

She looks the guest-wannabe in the eye and says, sincerely and regretfully, "I wish everyone could be included, but that is not possible."

IS THIS AN OFFICE OR A WEDDING?

Much of the ceremony surrounding a formal affair like a wedding involves pen and paper. The art of responding to an invitation with a formal, handwritten acceptance is being undermined by response cards and other pseudo-correct customs borrowed from the business world. Today's bride may find herself pressed for time, but she should resist the temptation to cut corners.

Here's what's what:

❤ Response cards have become acceptable, but they are not correct. Your guests should respond to your invitation with a hand-written note on their own stationery. Unfortunately, people no longer realize how important it is to have their own notepaper.

If you do decide to use response cards, they should look like this:

> _____
> Accept with pleasure
> Regret they cannot attend

The blank line is for names. Guests will then circle the appropriate phrase below it. Do not put "Number of guests" or "Number attending." Guests will assume that means they can invite as many people as they want.

Another graceful way of prompting lazy guests is to send a blank response card with "RSVP" in the left-hand corner. Guests will use these to write their own acceptances or regrets.

Response cards should be accompanied by stamped, self-addressed envelopes.

❤ In the movie *Working Girl*, big hair and heavy makeup labeled women as secretaries. Notes printed with the words "Thank You" will

> "*You know all that stuff I call men, 'hot slabs of meat,' 'love slaves,' 'pigs' — that's all affectionate.*"
>
> —Judy Tenuta, comedian

> *"Choose your words with taste. You may have to eat them."*
>
> —Graffiti

mark you as tacky. Don't use them. Instead, get quality notepaper printed with your name (or monogram) or plain foldover notes (a colored border is okay).

♥ Computers are great for helping you keep your guest list up to date, but don't use computer-generated labels on your invitations. Instead, write them by hand (no mistakes, please!).

BUDGET TIPS

♥ Some brides hire calligraphers to address their invitations. It's a nice touch but not necessary. Save money by asking your bridesmaids to an address-the-invitations party instead.

♥ At one time, tissue was inserted in engraved invitations to keep the oil-based inks from smearing. Today's water-based inks are quicker drying, and this is no longer a problem. Invitations printed by thermography don't need tissue either. Don't use it if you don't need it. Stationery stores and printers charge for it. Besides, it looks affected.

Wedding Arithmetic

ooooo

Most couples begin planning their wedding backwards: with the amount of money they have to spend or the number of people who can be served at the reception.

Couples should start with the guest list. That list should include—not your mother's college roommate whom you've never met, nor your father's boss—but the people who mean more to you than anyone else in the world. The list should have the names of the people whose love and support you two want as you pledge to spend the rest of your lives together.

Then figure out what you can afford to serve them and where. Your friends and family—not your menu, not your entertainment—should be your first consideration. People are

more important than being able to serve shrimp and roast beef.

PESKY PROBLEMS

💗 Although the wedding invitation is issued by your parents, you can use your address for the RSVP if you are keeping track of the responses. Guests will mail their gifts to your address as well.

💗 If the wedding does not take place in a church—if, for instance, you are getting married at home or in a hotel—the words "the honour of your presence" would be replaced by "the pleasure of your company."

💗 The times of the ceremony and the reception are written out: at eight o'clock in evening; at half after five o'clock. Weddings are not held on the quarter hour—like 5:15 or quarter till six—and "a.m." and "p.m." are never used.

💜 You need not write out the address if the wedding or reception site is a well-known landmark. But you do need to list the city—and the state if you are being married in a small town.

💜 You need not include the year, except on a wedding anouncement.

💜 Do not use nicknames or initials. Use complete whole names on the invitation—unless your bridegroom threatens to call off the wedding if you reveal what his middle name is.

DO-IT-YOURSELF INVITATIONS

If you are having an intimate wedding, you do not have to go through all the expense of engraving. You may write your invitations yourself in black or blue-black ink on quality paper. This is very proper and looks quite elegant. But, none of those "You are invited" cards from the drug store, please!

WE DID IT!

Couples who have intimate weddings find that formal announcements are a good way to share their news with friends and family. This also works for couples who elope.

Just don't do as one couple did: They sent a sentimental poem announcing their elopement. Too bad all their friends knew that the bride and groom were having an affair while he was married to someone else.

"*It is possible that blondes also prefer gentlemen.*"

—Mamie Van Doren
American Actress

3
My Wedding Must Be Perfect Because It's "My Day"

Here Comes the Bride

ooooo

Weddings have become such productions that sometimes it seems as if more thought goes into picking the color of the bride's lipstick than into the marriage.

But The Wedding, this curious mix of religious ceremony and cocktail party, serves as a rite of passage to your new life together. Couples want to pledge their love with the blessing and support of their community, their family, their friends. The wedding is only the first step; the marriage afterwards is their goal.

Sometimes people become so wrapped up in planning a "perfect" wedding, in having "the wedding of their dreams," that they lose sight of the goal: creating a new family from two established ones. If you find yourself becoming overwhelmed by your wedding preparations, stop and ask, "What's important? In five years, in fifteen, what do I want to remember about my wedding day?"

Don't go overboard with video-taping your wedding. One couple not only had three cameras going inside the church, but a camera-man backed down the aisle in front of the bride as he taped her making her grand entrance.

Theme Weddings

ooooo

GOOD IDEAS:

❤ Victorian or medieval theme wedding: The bride gets to wear a great dress.

❤ Horseback wedding: The bride gets to wear a riding habit.

❤ Western barbecue and square dance: The groom gets to wear jeans.

BAD IDEAS:

❤ Getting married in the snack aisle at a convenience market: How do you find romance between the potato chips and the motor oil?

♥ Getting married in a Moonie ceremony with hundreds of other couples: There's no way to make it "your" special day.

♥ Having fifteen bridesmaids. You'll look like a homecoming queen.

HUNKA, HUNKA BURNING LOVE AND OTHER OFFBEAT WEDDINGS

White tulle wedding gowns and a dozen bridesmaids aren't for everyone. A formal ceremony cramps some couples' style, so they create their own wedding theme. I see these as offbeat rather than tacky, because these people are not trying to be anything but themselves.

♥ An Atlanta couple went to Las Vegas to get married in the Graceland Chapel, named such with the King's personal blessing. The bride, an artist, painted scenes commemorating Elvis' life on her long, black velvet sheath. Her husband wore an Elvis outfit, but the best part was the minister. Wearing a Fat Elvis white jumpsuit and cape, he serenaded the newlyweds with "Can't Help Falling in Love."

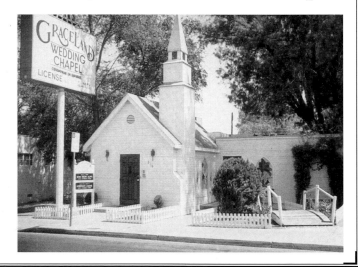

♥ Two Humane Society members in Oregon walked down the aisle accompanied by a flower girl and ring bearer with cold noses: their dogs.

> *"I was on the corner the other day when this wild-looking sort of gypsy lady with a dark veil over her face grabbed me right on Ventura Boulevard and said, 'Karen Haber! You're never going to find happiness, and no one is ever going to marry you.' I said, 'Mom, leave me alone.'"*
>
> —Karen Haber, comedian

♥ A motorcycle-loving couple in Atlanta got married on the finish line of the Atlanta Motor Speedway. The groom arrived on the back of a Kawasaki bike, and the bride wore her pink motorcycle boots beneath her rented pink gown. Her going-away clothes were pink and white racing leathers.

♥ An Indiana bride wore ruby-red slippers as she walked down a "yellow brick road" aisle runner.

♥ One Georgia couple, whose hobby is Civil War reenactments, dressed in 1860s costumes. The guests and wedding party wore Southern-belle dresses and Confederate uniforms.

♥ A Dallas bride who is an artist was married at her home. Before the ceremony, the wedding guests were invited to paint a mural celebrating life and love.

❤ An older couple borrowed traditions from Native American ceremonies for their wedding. Their children and close friends stood in a circle surrounding them. As they passed a spirit stick around the circle, each person offered advice, favorite sayings, and blessings for the couple.

❤ One Tennessee couple, who met while hiking, got married on their favorite mountain. The groom wore a tuxedo and the bride a formal white gown, but she was barefoot. She had forgotten her shoes!

❤ A North Carolina couple who like to fly fish married in Montana. Their wedding was in a rural chapel so tiny that the bride's train stretched out the door. Since there was no organ, their six guests hummed "Here Comes the Bride." Thirty minutes after the ceremony, the groom, his tux pants tucked into waders, was again fishing on the river.

💙 One couple, who had married on a Caribbean island, invited guests to a party after they returned. As guests watched a video of the wedding, the couple sneaked into the darkened room. When the lights came up, there they were, dressed in their wedding fin-

ery, looking as though they had stepped out of the video.

💙 One Atlanta man surprised his girlfriend at breakfast with a wedding ring and a proposal to get married—that day! A limo arrived and whisked them to get their blood tests and wedding license. Then it was off to the mall, where they bought their wedding clothes. The bride had her makeup done at the Chanel counter at Neiman Marcus. They used the car phone to invite their shocked families and friends to their four o'clock wedding. The chauffeur surprised them with a bottle of champagne. After the wedding, everyone dined at the couple's favorite restaurant. They even had a wedding cake, supplied by a Nashville friend who hopped on a plane to attend the impromptu affair.

> *"When marriage is outlawed, only outlaws will have in-laws."*
>
> —Graffiti

ON THE OTHER HAND, THESE ARE TACKY

💜 A couple who married in Jamaica sent their wedding photo to their hometown newspaper: It showed the barefoot twosome sitting on a rock, the ocean behind them. According to the story, the bride's white wedding bikini was designed by Barely Visible.

💜 In Alaska, a member of the National Rifle Association exchanged pistols with his bride instead of rings.

💜 An Alabama bride dressed her bridesmaids in look-alike Scarlett barbecue dresses for her *Gone With the Wind* theme wedding. But what really had guests tittering was the Tara backdrop set up behind the altar.

Trying to inject fun into her church wedding, one bride had her attendants come down the aisle in sunglasses. The groomsmen wore Hawaiian ties. It didn't work. What was supposed to seem spontaneous looked planned. Ditto for the couple who wore bathing suits under their wedding clothes. They stripped off their formal clothes at their reception and jumped into the swimming pool.

ONLY IN VEGAS

The Wedding Chapels in Las Vegas advertise that "One celebrity liked our chapels so much, she plans to have all her weddings here."

The Little White Chapel promises "We Never Close!" and advertises that Joan Collins and Michael Jordan were married there (not to each other!). The chapel features the one and

A bride who was obviously a frustrated ballerina came down the aisle en pointe in her toe shoes. She twirled around in a pirouette as she reached the groom.

only Drive-Up Wedding Window, where couples say I do without leaving the comfort of their car.

GET WITH THE PROGRAM

A program for your wedding guests isn't necessary, but if your ceremony contains a lot of wonderful music, you may wish to have one so guests will know what they are hearing. Programs get ridiculous when they include superfluous information about the wedding party. Don't ever fall into this tackiness trap, as this bride did: the back of her program had a list of the guests and where they were from.

Tacky Tunes

○○○○○

♥ "Daddy's Little Girl"

♥ Anything by Chicago

♥ "One Heart, One Soul"

♥ "The Way You Look Tonight"

♥ "You'll Never Walk Alone"

♥ "Bridge Over Troubled Water"

♥ "Theme from *Rocky*"

(These were actually heard at real weddings.)

OFF-KEY WEDDING NOTES

❖ One pastor recalls the worst song he'd ever heard, Carly Simon's "I Feel the Earth Move." The soloist cut loose just as the minister pronounced the couple husband and wife.

❖ One wedding guest was startled by the mix of music at one West Virginia ceremony: after being soothed by the very traditional "Ode to Joy" and Pachelbel's Canon in D, she was jolted by three country music tunes.

❖ As one woman complained, "It's not just the music, it's the soloists who can't sing."

IT'S SIMPLY NOT DONE

The groom who serenades his bride (and vice versa).

TACKY BUDGET TIP

Don't replace the organist with a boom box.

TACKY TRENDS

♥ Honoring dead parents.

♥ The audience stands as the bride enters (clue: she's not royalty).

♥ The minister "presenting" the happy couple as Mr. and Mrs. at the altar.

♥ A clapping congregation.

♥ The bride and groom "dismissing" the congregation one row at a time (that's a job for the ushers).

GREAT WEDDING IDEAS

♥ Using customs from other lands. African-American couples jump the broom, for instance, as they leave the altar to bless their new household. Hispanic grooms may give their brides thirteen gold coins to ensure prosperity.

♥ Writing your own vows and memorizing them instead of repeating them. Couples often find that the soul-searching needed during the writing brings them closer together.

♥ Borrowing a custom from Jewish weddings and having both parents escort the bride and the groom to the altar.

♥ Asking members of your families to perform special readings.

♥ Wearing something that links you to a loved one. Many brides wear their mothers' gowns. One groom said carrying his late father's pocket watch "made me feel like I had him with me."

♥ Having all children as the bride's attendants.

♥ Including your children in the ceremony at a second marriage.

IT'S A SMALL WORLD

"Blest be the tie that binds," goes the old hymn, and the tie that binds in marriage today is as varied as the people it unites. The world is a much smaller place, and many taboos against people of different races or religions marrying are falling away. One Cleveland wedding was a white-tulle melting pot, bringing together a Greek Orthodox bride, a Protestant groom, a Japanese-American bridesmaid, and African-American friends in the congregation.

But a wedding that crosses these lines can be a minefield of slights and misunderstandings. At a Protestant-Jewish marriage, the groom's family and guests were insulted when a soloist sang "Ave Maria." Work closely with your minister, priest, or rabbi to avoid these mistakes.

THE SECOND — OR THIRD — TIME AROUND

Let's face it: divorce looms as a large, ugly statistic in modern society. Most of us have been touched by its cold hand, and rare today is the family no man has put asunder. Many brides and grooms are marrying for the second—and last, I hope—time. Many of them worry about what's "proper" and "doing the right thing."

Should the bride wear white? May the groom have a bachelor party? Should the same people be asked to be bridesmaids and groomsmen one more time? Is it okay for the couple's children to be in the ceremony?

In the days where divorce was taboo, a bride's second wedding was so low-key that she didn't even feel like she was getting married. Some churches refused to allow music at second weddings, and children in the ceremony were considered gauche. It was as if the happy couple had to sneak to get married.

Today, second-time brides are being told that "anything goes!" While I don't agree with this extreme—after all, not many of your friends will want to ante up for yet another bridesmaid dress—I do think second, and even third, weddings should be a cause for celebration, rejoicing, and hope. Just do it tastefully.

The key here is moderation with the emphasis on family. Have a small ceremony with a party for your friends afterwards. No big church ceremony with scads of bridesmaids and hundreds of guests. No big white gown with ruffles and a train.

> "*My mother says she just wants me to be happy — doing what she wants me to do.*"
>
> — Julia Wills, comedian

A white dress is okay, as long as it's accented in a pastel color, but a dressy evening suit is better. A veil should never be worn.

Attendants are acceptable, just not as many of them. And your children, of course, should be an important part of the ceremony.

Don't try to overdo it, and you just might find yourselves having more fun the second time around.

GREAT WEDDING MOVIES

- 💎 *Betsy's Wedding*
- 💎 *Four Weddings and a Funeral*
- 💎 *Steel Magnolias*
- 💎 *Father of the Bride*—both versions

One bride argued that she deserved a large wedding because even though this was her second marriage, it was the first time she'd picked the right man.

TACKY TREND

Sociologists now call marriages that last less than two or three years "starter marriages." Brides planning a second marriage argue that those "practice marriages" didn't count. Wrong. They do.

IT'S TIME TO RETIRE:

- ❤ Those backless black polyester bridesmaids dresses with the ropes of pearls

- ❤ "The Wedding Song"

- ❤ Invitations that say, "This day I will marry my best friend, the one I laugh with, live for, dream with, love."

- ❤ Pillbox hats à la Jackie O.

LETTER FROM A REAL BRIDE: My fiancé and I are having an informal wedding of about 100 guests. My parents are deceased. I have never cared for the tradition of the bride being escorted down the aisle to the groom. However, I have two brothers I would like to include in the ceremony. I would like for the processional to be our whole families: my brothers, their wives, my fiancé's brother and his wife, and my fiancé's parents. They would be followed by our maid of honor and our best man. Then my fiancé and I would walk in together. This has raised a few eyebrows. — IN-STEP

DEAR IN-STEP: I bet it has, but I love the idea. You are merely taking the idea of parents and grandparents participating in the Jewish wedding ceremony and expanding it. For someone who has lost her parents, it is a wonderful way of showing how important family is and who really matters in her life.

Here Comes the Bride: Kidstuff

ᴏᴏᴏᴏᴏ

When it comes to children and weddings, adults can act very childish. The biggest problem is parents who bring their uninvited children to the wedding, sure that everyone would just love to see their little darlings. Wrong! Many brides do not want children at their weddings because A) children today are so ill-behaved or B) they have planned an elegant reception that is no place for kids.

Unfortunately, some brides have resorted to putting a highly improper "Adults only" on their invitations. These admonitions are tacky. If you do not want children at your wedding, the proper thing to do is not invite them.

If there are any parents who might ignore this, reinforce your message in person or writing: "Gee, I sure wish we could include the children, but we just can't" (you need not explain why). Enlist your mother and other relatives to get out the word.

Bring up the issue before the doting parents can: "We wanted this to be a grown-up affair so parents could have fun without worrying about their little ones." (You will be surprised how many parents will welcome this!)

As a last resort, plan to have a nursery. Any parent brazen enough to try to smuggle in anyone under three feet tall can be directed there by the ushers.

COULD WE SEE AN I.D., PLEASE?

Just how old are flower girls and ring bearers supposed to be, anyway? Many books put age limits—between 4 and 7 years—but 10 is not too old. The only

TOO TACKY FOR WORDS

- Guests bringing their uninvited children to a wedding.

- Putting "Adults-only reception" on your wedding invitation.

- Miniature brides and grooms.

- Little bitty tuxes on ring bearers.

- Not inviting the flower girl or the ring bearer to the reception because "it's just for adults."

requirement is that the child be someone special in your life.

And there is no law written in stone from the Great Etiquette God that says the ring bearer can't be a girl and the flower girl can't be a boy. After all, girls can now play Little League.

"I'm the Bride in My Mother's Wedding"

ooooo

When it comes to weddings, everyone is a critic. Everyone—no matter how limited his or her experience—has expectations of what a wedding should be and feels free to express those opinions frequently and loudly. Sometimes the bride and the groom end up feeling it's not their wedding at all. A group of newly married friends in Chicago unanimously summed up their nuptial experiences as "I'm the bride in my mother's wedding."

One California mother, usually a perfectly sane woman and a delight to be around, became so obsessed with her daughter's plans that the couple eloped. Another mother was overheard telling her daughter in the bridal salon dressing room: "I'm paying for this wedding, and you'll wear what I tell you to wear."

Although mothers seem to be the biggest culprits, fathers (and stepmothers!) aren't immune from tackiness. Here are some real parent traps:

USING THEIR DAUGHTER'S WEDDING AS PAY-BACK TIME

♥ All too often mothers and fathers see a wedding as their one chance to return the hospitality of any invitations they have accepted in the past thirty years. The poor bride and groom find themselves in a receiving line with hundreds of strangers eager to get to the bar. These people could care less about the couple's happiness. All they want is a drink.

○○○○○

> "The music at a wedding procession always reminds me of the music of soldiers going into battle."
>
> —Henrich Heine, German poet

THIS WEDDING HAS TO BE "PERFECT"

♥ Call it Martha's Wedding Anxiety Theory No. 1: Planning a wedding has become so stressful because people no longer entertain regularly. They see their wedding as their one chance to host a great party, convincing themselves that nothing will go wrong. Not! Something's always going to go wrong.

If people entertained regularly, they wouldn't sweat the small stuff when it comes to a wedding. They would take missing shoes, drooping candles, and sagging cakes in stride. After all, having a wedding isn't brain surgery.

HAVING A MEGA-WEDDING TO IMPRESS PEOPLE

Going into debt to hold a lavish wedding simply to impress people is crazy—and a bad investment. Remember, half of today's marriages end in divorce.

OBSESSING OVER WHO PAYS FOR WHAT

When divorced parents split their worldly goods, they also split the payments for their children's weddings. This can lead to arguments over who gets top billing on the wedding invitations.

FYI: A wedding invitation should not be a guide to who is a $15,000 sponsor and who is a $500 sponsor. Just because Papa is footing most of the bills doesn't mean his name should go on top. Etiquette says the parent who raised the bride should issue the wedding invitations. If the parents are divorced and want both names on the invitation, the mother's goes first—no matter who is paying for the wedding.

One Dallas socialite had to sell her house and move into a condominium after her daughter's mega-wedding.

USING THE WEDDING TO GET BACK AT YOUR EX

Unfortunately, acrimonious divorces are a fact of modern life. But it's sad when grown-ups can't put aside their differences for the six hours it takes to marry off their children. More than one mother of the bride has threatened not to attend the wedding if her ex-husband's new wife is there. Just as bad is the mother who urged her daughter to plan an extravagant wedding—at her ex-husband's expense.

ACTING LIKE CHILDREN

♥ The mother who was sure her daughter's wedding would be ruined because the groom's father insisted on wearing his own, three-year-old tuxedo instead of renting a new one.

♥ The groom's mother who refused to come to the reception unless she could smoke.

♥ The mother who was hurt because her daughter was not wearing her wedding dress.

♥ The groom's mother who insisted on adding more flowers of her own choosing to the altar decorations.

It's hard to believe that people get upset over such trivial issues, but they do. And these bad feelings can taint family relationships for years. A Birmingham woman was among the fifty guests at a small wedding with feuding parents. At the reception, the families sat on opposite sides of the hall, refusing to speak to each other. "Until the bride and groom got there, it was dead silence," the guest recalled.

THE WICKED STEPMOTHER

💜 The stepmother who insists on sitting in the first pew, a spot reserved for the mothers of the bride and groom.

💜 The stepmother who refuses to let the groom's half-sister be a flower girl because, with three other flower girls in the wedding, it wouldn't be a special honor for her daughter.

💜 The stepmother who didn't want her husband's daughters from his first marriage to be bridesmaids in their daughter's wedding.

💜 The stepmother who resents the bride's relationship with her father.

Too many times weddings become a competition between the old and the new families. Stepmothers should keep a low profile and not expect to be in all of the family photos.

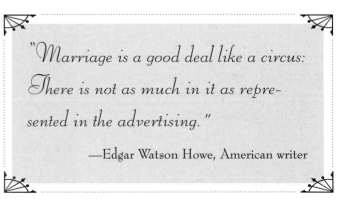

"Marriage is a good deal like a circus: There is not as much in it as represented in the advertising."

—Edgar Watson Howe, American writer

BLAME IT ON SNOW WHITE'S EVIL STEPMOTHER

LETTER FROM A REAL BRIDE: My father is married to a woman I strongly dislike. Over the past ten years, I have been civil to her at my father's request, but the situation remains very stormy. None of the rest of my family can tolerate her either. I want my wedding to be a happy event, and I don't want my father's wife to ruin it. My fiancé says don't invite her.—SCARED OF STEPMONSTER

DEAR SCARED: What do you think she will do, protest the marriage? Throw wedding cake? Hog all the dances with the groom?

If she is someone you think will cause a disturbance, leave her off your guest list. But you cannot expect your father to attend without her.

If you are worried about where she is to sit, she should be seated toward the rear of the church. At the reception, neither she nor your father need be included in the receiving line.

SWEET REVENGE

After many hours of shopping, the mother of the bride finally found the perfect dress. To the bride's dismay, her stepmother—a trophy wife—chose the same gown and refused to wear anything else. So the mother of the bride gracefully headed back to the mall, where she found another outfit. What did she do with the first dress? "I wore it to the rehearsal dinner," she said sweetly. (*Reader's Digest*, November 1994)

"My mother can recite every gift we ever got — and who gave it to us," says a woman who's been married for ten years. "What's more, she can tell you every wedding gift she ever got."

D-I-V-O-R-C-E

What's the biggest problem with getting married today? That ugly "D" word, divorce. I'm not talking about the newlyweds and the danger of future problems between them. It's those divorces from the past that haunt families: their parents' or even their grandparents'.

Planning a wedding gets sticky when the bride has to juggle where divorced-yet-still-feuding parents will sit. Whether parents can be trusted to stand in the receiving line without sniping at each other. Whether they can be posed together for a family portrait without a new wife or husband getting jealous.

Unfortunately, parents don't always act like grown-ups. They let their anger and bitterness poison what should be a joyous occasion. No bride or groom should have to suffer that. A wedding day is the one time estranged parents should put aside their animosities and put their children's feelings first. That would be the best wedding gift of all.

As the bride's mother kept making snide remarks about the gown her daughter had selected, the salon owner lost her cool. "This dress," she said, "was made in New York City, not heaven."

FAMILY AFFAIRS

◈ By the wedding day, no one was speaking. At the reception in a posh Atlanta hotel, the mothers got into a fistfight that looked like "Championship Wrestling" on TV.

◈ At the rehearsal dinner, the father of the groom announced that he was giving his son a $1 million trust fund. "What was really great was the minister," said a guest. "He said, 'A-men!'"

◈ The groom's mother sent wedding announcements to the local newspapers, but she didn't bother to include the names of the bride's parents.

One bride forgot her shoes and had to wear her running shoes. The groom — and his parents — was so appalled, he almost called off the wedding.

"BRIDESMAIDS FROM HELL"

When a bride asks them to be in her wedding, somehow these women are transformed from bosom buddies to bitch bridesmaids.

Here are some of the evil things they do:

 Complain about the style and color of their outfits

- ❤ Lie about their sizes

- ❤ Complain about the price

- ❤ "Forget" to reimburse the bride for their outfits

- ❤ Expect the bride to set them up with eligible groomsmen

- ❤ Flirt with married groomsmen

- ❤ Don't give the bride a shower

- ❤ Get VERY pregnant and refuse to relinquish their spot as a bridesmaid

- ❤ Sleep with the groom

THE BRIDESMAID'S TALE

💎 Several bridesmaids disappeared into the ladies' room during a reception at a posh Nashville wedding. When they returned, they were wearing miniskirts. They had cut off their gowns.

💎 One bridesmaid spent too much time in the tanning bed the night before her brother's winter wedding. In the wedding photos, she's so artificially dark, all you see are her teeth.

💎 The trip to the beauty salon before this New York wedding was supposed to be relaxing, but one bridesmaid got so upset about the way her hair was styled, she insisted on having it redone. She took so much of the hairdresser's time that the bride had to do her own hair.

GOOD ADVICE:

"The more people you have in your wedding whom you aren't close to, the more trouble you're going to have."—A wedding consultant who wishes to remain anonymous

"It's considered bad luck for the real bride to walk down the aisle at rehearsal. We hear it's sometimes done by girls in the North, but in the South, that's just tempting fate."—Maryln Schwartz, *New Money in the Old South*

FROM SOUTHERN BELLE TO BRIDESMAID

"Just getting the bridesmaids to act as a unit is somewhat like training for the Rockettes. Everything is done with precision. Southern bridesmaids must wear their hair in the exact same style when walking down the aisle, and they must have it done by the exact same hairdresser. The same goes for their makeup, the color of their nails, the color of their lipstick, and the color of their shoes, which they dye exactly to match the color of their gowns."—Maryln Schwartz, *New Money in the Old South*

BRIDESMAIDS HATE WASTING THEIR MONEY ON:

◆ Ugly polyester dresses in colors not found in nature

◆ Satin gloves dyed to match

◆ Hats with netting

◆ Gloves sprinkled with rhinestones

◆ Dyed pumps

"You Can't Get Married Again . . . and Again"

◦◦◦◦◦

What happens when couples want to say, "I do" all over again? Reaffirmation of vows, commonly known "renewing our vows," has long been a religious rite.

These loving ceremonies—when a couple promises that they would marry each other all over again, despite kids, bills, and mortgages—are held on a major anniversary, such as the twenty-fifth. They are simple affairs, often taking place during a regular service at their church. The couple wears their Sunday best, and their children may stand with them.

Unfortunately some couples are using these religious ceremonies as a chance to have a "second wedding," complete with bridesmaids, a fabulous gown, and lots of presents. Etiquette's answer is always the same: You are married. You cannot have a "wedding." You cannot go back to bridesmaids and white gowns. Have a big anniversary party with flowers, a band, and lots of champagne instead. What you are planning is quite tacky.

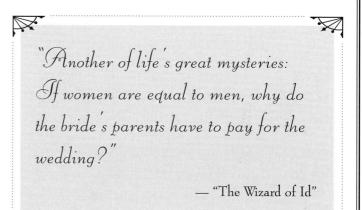

"Another of life's great mysteries: If women are equal to men, why do the bride's parents have to pay for the wedding?"

— "The Wizard of Id"

> *"Nothing so surely produces a sour note into a wedding ceremony as the abrupt disappearance of the groom in a cloud of dust."*
>
> —P. G. Wodehouse, British humorist

An exception may be made for the couple who married in a civil ceremony in times of war or family illness. They may have a quiet church wedding within a year of their civil marriage.

Weddings are a unique blend of religious, civil, and social ceremonies. A wedding service is a religious rite, not a social right. Couples who want to be the center of attention at a fab-ulous event should throw themselves a terrific anniversary party and dance the night away.

"I WANT TO RENEW OUR VOWS BECAUSE..."

♥ I didn't get the wedding I wanted first time around.

♥ I want to wear a beautiful long, white gown.

♥ We eloped, and no one gave us any presents.

♥ I'm tired of my china pattern.

♥ We couldn't afford a wedding with "all the trimmings."

♥ I hate our wedding pictures.

- ♥ My children want to see Mommy as a bride.

- ♥ Our wedding consultant was mean and wouldn't let us do what we wanted.

- ♥ Everyone will have to tell me how beautiful I am.

- ♥ I deserve it.

> *"My true friends have always given me that supreme proof of devotion, a spontaneous aversion for the man I loved."*
>
> —Colette, French writer

TOO TACKY FOR WORDS

One North Carolina bride, whose mother was happily planning a large spring wedding, surprised her family: She and her boyfriend couldn't wait till June so they had a quickie courthouse ceremony. When her mother lamented that now she couldn't give her daughter a wedding, the bride insisted she still wanted to have the elaborate ceremony, complete with eight bridesmaids. Just because she was married, said the newlywed, didn't mean that she couldn't have the wedding of her dreams.

Toasts of the Town

ooooo

Just like in the song, the reception is *your* party. It's your time to shine, to have fun, to revel in the good wishes of your friends and family.

But a reception is just like any other party in one way: guests will remember the good times fondly, but any faux pas will become part of their comedy repertoire forever. Here are some mistakes other brides made but you will surely avoid:

INVITING GUESTS TO AN EVENING WEDDING AND THEN JUST SERVING CAKE AND PUNCH

♥ When your reception takes place dictates the type of affair you will hold. Guests take their cues from this. For example, if you have a 6:00 p.m. wedding, they know that the reception will be their evening meal, whether it's a buffet or a seated affair.

If your budget allows only cake and punch, then you are having a reception that should be held at 3:00 or 4:00 in the afternoon.

LETTER FROM A REAL BRIDE: I am planning a wedding reception for approximately 250 guests. The catering company will charge me $15 per guest. Because of this, we are planning an "adults only" reception. I thought of enclosing a brief note along with the invitation to explain. Here is an example:

Dear Guests,

Please note that the reception is "adults only." Due to economical reasons, children are excluded since the catering company is charging a fee per person. We deeply regret this decision since we would love to have children share the celebration of this occasion. We hope you will be understanding about our painful decision.

Sincerely,
The Bride and Groom

Would this note be considered proper etiquette?—PINCHING PENNIES

DEAR PINCHING: No. You don't invite someone to a party by notifying them you are spending money on them.

ASKING GUESTS TO MARK THEIR CHOICE OF ENTRÉE ON THE RESPONSE CARD

You're not running a restaurant. It is extremely tacky to have spaces to check roast beef or chicken on the response card. Instead, have the caterer serve small portions of each entrée artfully arranged on the same plate.

SCHEDULING THE RECEPTION MORE THAN THIRTY MINUTES AFTER THE CEREMONY

A tacky trend is holding receptions three or four hours after the wedding. A reception should always take place "immediately" after the ceremony. Leaving guests all dressed up with no place to go for several hours inconveniences them, which is inexcusably rude.

HAVING A RECEIVING LINE / NOT HAVING A RECEIVING LINE

If you are having a big wedding, making all 500 or so guests wait to enter the reception is rude. Form your receiving line in another part of the room so guests can approach you instead of making it a gauntlet they have to run to get in the front door.

Many brides do not like the idea of a receiving line, but a short one, of the couple and their mothers, is the best and most efficient method of making sure you speak to each guest.

HAVING A CASH BAR AT A RECEPTION

Inviting guests to a wedding reception is the same as entertaining them in your home. You wouldn't ask someone to pay for a glass of wine or scotch in your living room, so don't even think about doing it at your reception.

If you cannot afford to offer alcoholic drinks, none should be available. Expecting guests to pay their way is extremely tacky.

NO PLACE FOR PRACTICAL JOKES

No matter how strong the temptation, please refrain from smashing the wedding cake into each other's faces. And pity the poor bride whose groom pretended to pull off her bikini panties instead of her garter. A wedding should be a happy, joyous celebration, so hijinks that might hurt feelings or embarrass someone are not appropriate.

> *At the end of dinner, it used to be that the men would retire to the billiard room and the women would go into the parlor. Men and women no longer separate after dinner, however. They now separate after twenty years of apparently happy marriage.*
>
> —P. J. O'Rourke, American humorist

BRIDAL PANTY RAID

The *Atlanta Journal-Constitution* received this wedding story. The names have been changed to protect the truly tacky:

"Following the wedding of Curt Bookman and Sandra Maynard last Saturday, the bridegroom reached for the garter and came out with . . . panties! (Some people think it was a joke.) Bookman, 32 and not previously married, apparently has had a lot of experience."

SINKING HIS TEETH INTO MARRIAGE

"During the garter ceremony at our reception, Bill thought he would be cute," says Joan, a New Jersey bride. "He pulled off the garter with his teeth. Everyone laughed, but I was mortified."

OPENING GIFTS AT THE RECEPTION

Not everyone knows that gifts should be delivered to the bride's home, so you may be surprised by well-meaning guests handing you a wrapped package at the reception. Thank the giver, mentioning that you and your new spouse will open it later together. Don't feel you have to open it then and there.

> *"Couples who cook together stay together. (Maybe because they can't decide who'll get the Cuisinart.)"*
>
> —Erica Jong, American novelist

TURNING THE FESTIVITIES INTO A JOINT WEDDING RECEPTION–BABY SHOWER

A tacky trend in some Mississippi Baptist churches is to show off the couple's baby at their wedding reception. On the other hand, at least the parents got married.

PUTTING OUT "NO SMOKING" SIGNS

Most smokers realize that their habit is socially unacceptable and will go outdoors, however grudgingly, to indulge themselves. Many public places today are smoke-free, and the absence of ashtrays at the reception will be a clear clue that you do not want people to smoke. But if you are afraid that someone is too loutish to take the hint, put a small "no smoking, please" sign in a beautiful script by the guest register.

Do not even begin to think about putting "no smoking" warnings on your wedding invitations.

HAVING AN ECOLOGICALLY UNAWARE RECEPTION

You don't have to go so far as to have your invitations printed on recycled paper with soya ink, but some couples thoughtlessly harm the environment with some of the cutesy things they do. Toss birdseed instead of dimestore glitter, for example. Don't give your guests balloons to release as you leave. The balloons can travel hundreds of miles, coming to earth in pristine areas or in the ocean, where sea turtles mistake them for food.

The owners of a historic Savannah house that was often used for receptions finally had to bar couples from releasing doves. "We had doves everywhere," they said. "And they didn't know how to live in the wild. It was horrible because most of them died."

TACKY TRENDS

♥ Cheap pink champagne

♥ Champagne fountains

- Wheeling the many-tiered wedding cake in with a drumroll and a spotlight

- The couple dancing alone as waiters hoisting flaming desserts march in and surround them

- A parade of waiters carrying oversize bottles of champagne for a toast to the happy couple

- The couple smashing cake into each other's faces

- A 16- by 20-inch color photograph of the bride by the guest book

- Releasing doves

TACKY BUDGET TIPS YOU'LL REGRET

⬦ Expecting guests to help themselves to roast beef instead of hiring a carver.

⬦ Asking your cousin, who likes to take pictures, to act as wedding photographer. One bride ended up with photos just of the people the photographer knew.

⬦ Relying on a friend to make your wedding cake.

⬦ Skimping on the reception so you can afford a video.

⬦ Holding the reception in the church recreation hall. Even if you decorate the basketball hoops with streamers, your reception will still look like a prom.

⬦ Skimping on food and drink so you can have a more expensive gown and flowers.

A guest at a small-town wedding couldn't believe the buffet at the reception: The lasagna was served in the pan it baked in, and bottles of dressing were set next to the salad.

TIPS THAT YOU'VE HIRED A TACKY CATERER

- ◆ The crackers are in cellophane packages.
- ◆ The fish is frozen.
- ◆ The waiters are wearing shorts.
- ◆ The napkins have the caterer's name, not yours.

GROOM'S CAKES

One cake is not enough at weddings these days. The groom gets a cake of his own, and brides think it's fun to have the cake look like her darling's favorite pastime:

♥ A chocolate choo-choo

♥ Animals like ducks and armadillos

♥ His favorite team's colors

♥ A cross

♥ A pickup truck

♥ A map of Mississippi

WEDDING CAKES THAT FALL FLAT

◈ Cakes with bridges between the sections, and on the bridges, little brides maid and usher figurines.

◈ Precious Moments cake toppers

◈ Cakes with fountains

◈ Wedding cakes so tall that most of the layers are Styrofoam

"You two do know each other, don't you?"—Clever way to disguise the fact that you have forgotten someone's name.

KIDS KEEP OUT

One bride wanted to enlist her wedding party to help pass the word that children were not invited to the ceremony or reception. Mincing no words, she sent this letter:

When a formal invitation is sent out with Mr. and Mrs. Paul Smith on the outside of the envelope and Mr. and Mrs. Smith on the inside envelope, that is exactly what it means—only Mr. and Mrs. Smith are being invited and no one else, no others in the family, no guests who may be visiting at the time, etc.

I know it sounds like I am a real fusspot, but I would hate to tell you what the cost is per person just for the reception alone. I am doing all of this for my friends and relatives, for all of us to have a good time.

WHO HAS THE HONOR OF BANKROLLING THIS WEDDING?

One guest couldn't decide whether to laugh or cry when he was invited to a wedding that had an admission price. "Under the RSVP, the couple had included a monetary amount, $50 per person, with the note, 'Includes dinner, dancing and gift,'" he says. He didn't bother to attend.

"Maybe I am old-fashioned," says one older lady, "but I think it's just plain tacky to pass the hat at a wedding reception. A member of the bride's family actually passed a straw hat, decorated with flowers and ribbons, saying it was for donations for the couple's honeymoon."

One mother of the bride was so angered by people who said they were coming to the wedding and then didn't show up that she sent them a bill!

One bride had her groom's cake iced with the words: "All my money is my money, and all his money is my money, too."

SPENDING OTHER PEOPLE'S MONEY

LETTER FROM A REAL BRIDE: My fiancé and I are on a strict budget for our wedding. We want to keep our guest list to 150 people, but my fiancé's mother has pushed us over our limit. She has given me the names of relatives she hasn't seen or spoken to in years. I have never met any of these people, and many of them do not even know my fiancé is engaged.—FEELING PRESSURED

DEAR PRESSURED: Tell your future mother-in-law that you will mail wedding *announcements* to her family. These engraved

THRIFTY, BUT NOT TACKY

Can't afford an elaborate wedding reception? Here are some ways to save without being tacky:

- Invite just your family to the wedding and reception. Have a casual party for your friends after your honeymoon.

- Have your wedding on a Friday night or Sunday afternoon, when rental rates are lower.

- Have an afternoon reception with cake and simple finger foods. You won't need music either.

- Don't serve alcohol.

announcements go in the mail the day of the wedding and are the perfect, polite way to inform distant family and friends that a couple has married, particularly if they are on a tight budget.

LETTER FROM A REAL BRIDE: My parents generously agreed to assume all expenses for our wedding and reception—including the rehearsal dinner the night before. My problem is that my fiancé continues to insist that he wants a "sit-down" dinner at the reception for our 200 to 250 guests since this is his day, too, and he should have "what he wants." The proposed buffet is fabulous, but he says he is "unimpressed" and that if he can't have what he wants, he doesn't want to have anything to do with planning the reception. I am at a loss as how to appease him.—STRESSED BRIDE

DEAR STRESSED: Why should you have to appease this guy? *Your* parents are the hosts. It is their decision as to what their budget will allow, and it looks as if they very generously have planned an elegant evening for you. A buffet is quite appropriate and—take it from someone who has been to a million rubber chicken dinners—much tastier.

Now you see why I cringe when brides insist that a wedding is "my day" and they petulantly

> *"Social tact is making your company feel at home, even though you wish they were."*
>
> —Anonymous

demand that their desires be met. A gracious bride—and groom—puts others first, particularly when wallets are involved.

By the way, perhaps you need to think very hard about such an insensitive man who insists on spending someone else's money.

TOO TACKY FOR WORDS

The nursery rhyme tune that some bandleaders insist on playing as the happy couple cuts the cake:

> The bride cuts the cake,
> The bride cuts the cake,
> Hi-ho, the merrio, the bride cuts the cake.
> The bride feeds the groom,
> The bride feeds the groom,
> Hi-ho, the merrio, the bride feeds the groom.
> Etc. ad nauseum.

One Atlanta bride says she had the best wedding ever. The New York Mets were staying at the same hotel where her reception was being held. Her uncle bumped into the team in the lobby and invited them to the party. Everyone had a great time, and the bride got to meet Tom Seaver.

> "Consideration for others can mean taking a wing instead of a drumstick."
>
> —Garth Henrichs, writer

A bridesmaid at a South Carolina wedding says that after the cake-and-punch reception, everyone went out to dinner — at an all-you-can-eat fish camp. There she was, in her pink polyester lace dress, sitting at a picnic table. "The only thing tackier about that wedding was the divorce," she says. And yes, she had to pay for her meal herself.

REGIONAL SNOBBERY, OR THIS ISN'T THE WAY WE DO IT BACK HOME

When it comes to weddings, some families are fighting an Uncivil War. Wedding customs aren't the same all over the country.

In the North, for instance, receptions often are huge affairs with four-course dinners, alcoholic beverages, and a band. In the South, receptions can be as simple as a tea with cake and punch. Some religious groups ban alcohol and dancing, so Uncle Tony and Aunt Sophia from New Jersey might be in for a big shock when they attend a wedding in Montgomery, Alabama.

Some couples try to solve the problem by having two receptions, one in the bride's hometown, the other in the groom's. Still other couples try to incorporate some customs from both families.

LETTER FROM A REAL BRIDE: It has always been an understanding in our family that the groom's family paid for the rehearsal dinner and the liquor tab at the reception, even though all the etiquette books say the bride's family pays for the reception. For my wedding, my parents are having a large reception and want my fiancé's family to pay for the liquor, about $1,500 to $1,700. My fiancé's family says it has never heard of such a thing and accused my family of being "cheap." — BAMBOOZLED BRIDE

DEAR BAMBOOZLED: What other customs has your family made up lately? Traditionally, the bride's parents pick up *all* the expenses of the reception because they are the *hosts*. It is considered rude to *ask* the family of the groom, even if it is wealthier, to help pay for the reception. The bride's family limits a reception to what it can afford, whether that's a sit-down dinner for 200 or just an afternoon tea.

What you and your family must consider is that you will be dealing with these people long after the bar bill has been paid.

WRETCHED EXCESS

♥ In 1988, a wealthy New Yorker threw a wedding party for his daughter at the Metropolitan Museum of Art that cost about $3 million. The photographer was flown to New York two weeks before the wedding just to check the lighting.

♥ At another New York wedding held at the Plaza Hotel, guests were spotlit and announced as they entered the reception as if they were royalty. If the guest wasn't an easily recognizable name, his company was announced, too.

♥ One bride's family paid to have their church recarpeted in a color that complimented the bridesmaid dresses.

REHEARSAL DINNERS

♥ "I've been to some rehearsal dinners where the teasing gets pretty brutal," said a veteran groomsman. "At one, the best man showed a photo of the groom's old girlfriend and made the bride's mother cry."

♥ "Don't marry a man who refers to the rehearsal dinner as the Last Supper." — From *A Wife's Little Instruction Book*, by Diana Jordan and Paul Seaburn

♥ A Tennessee woman went to a rehearsal dinner that was held in a Morrison's Cafeteria. The wedding party went through the line, but the groom's family did pay for their meals.

Don't Rain on My Parade

ooooo

Showers are the one place brides and grooms can *expect* presents. The purpose of these little casual get-togethers is to help the couple furnish their household. The guests should be close friends and the gifts inexpensive.

Here are some guidelines:

♥ No one in the couple's family should host a shower. It looks greedy. Instead, the bride's friends (or friends of the couple's mothers) should host it.

♥ Bridesmaids are *not required* to host a shower for the bride, although it is a nice gesture.

♥ Limit yourself to one or two showers, please. Otherwise—you guessed it—it looks greedy.

♥ Don't invite the same people to each shower. You'll wipe out their wallets.

♥ If the bride already has a well-furnished household, she doesn't need to be showered, although a lingerie or a wine shower would be appropriate.

♥ Showers are *not* held for second marriages.

♥ Guests at showers should be invited to the wedding.

♥ If you are a wedding guest, you are not expected to send a gift to a shower to which you are not invited.

♥ Guests who cannot attend a shower do not need to send a gift.

♥ Showers are not just for the girls. The guys may be invited, too. Usually these showers are to furnish the bar, the garage, or the yard.

♥ Inviting the moms is not a requirement, but they like to be included.

THANK YOU VERY MUCH

A bride must always write her hostesses to thank them for the shower. This note should include thanks for their gift as well.

The bride need not write guests she thanked verbally at the shower. She must write anyone who did not attend but sent a gift anyway.

TACKY IDEAS

◈ The bride's family hosting a shower.

◈ A shower of cash.

◈ Showers where guests are expected to contribute to a group gift, whether they attend or not.

◈ Shower invitations that include a list of stores where the bride is registered.

A bride horrified her friends when she told them she wanted to have lots of showers so she could get lots of gifts.

One woman received an invitation to a tacky "shower by mail." There was no party. She was asked to send a gift that the bride would open at her leisure.

One tacky bride wanted to know how to word invitations to her shower and her fiancé's bachelor party. Hosting your own shower is bad enough, but this couple was planning to elope!

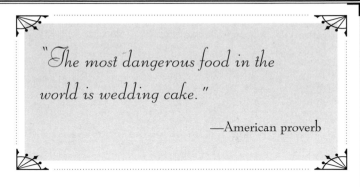

"The most dangerous food in the world is wedding cake."

—American proverb

TOO TACKY FOR WORDS

In Columbia, guests were invited to a shower that made them feel as if they were appearing on "The Price Is Right." The hostess told them not to bring gifts—because they could buy them at the party! The store where the couple had registered sent over items they had selected. These were arranged on a table, and guests were invited to purchase them for the bride, who was standing right there.

"I want you to come to the shower, but I don't know you well enough to invite you to the wedding," a bride-to-be told a Louisville woman. When the invitation arrived, the woman had been "assigned" to provide "something blue for the bathroom." Said the woman, "I took her a beautifully wrapped gift—a single roll of blue toilet paper."

The word "bridal" originally comes from the Old English words for "bride ale." Sometimes the bride would brew a strong ale—and sell it to her guests!

The word "husband" comes from the Old Norse words "hus" (house) and "boa" (to dwell). The origin of "wife" is uncertain. It may be derived from the Old Norse "vifathr," meaning veiled.

The origin of the word "bachelor" is disputed. It may be derived from "vacca," the Latin word for cow, meaning cowherd. Later it became the word for a young man who aspired to knighthood.

The word "spinster" meant a woman who could spin. Brides were expected to spin yarn for their trousseaus. A "spinster" was a woman still desperately trying to spin enough for her trousseau.

—*The Guinness Book of Marriage*

Gift Guide

∘∘∘∘∘

When couples start planning their weddings, it seems that one of the first questions is: How can we get people to give us what we want?

How, indeed? The most accepted way is the bridal registry, which allows couples to select china, silver, and crystal—both formal and everyday. These registries at local department and gift stores began as a service to brides—and to guests. The lists usually are for things that couples cannot afford, the sorts of items, says manners maven Letitia Baldrige, that couples fight over when they divorce.

But as American lifestyles have become more casual, brides and grooms often find they don't need all the fancy stuff their parents received. Others are the lucky beneficiaries of chests of family silver and china. They don't need more. What, they wail, are we to do?

Some couples have stooped to dreadful solutions. They stipulate on their wedding invitations that gifts of money are preferred. Others solicit contributions for their honeymoon or a new house. Some have even charged guests admission to the reception, which covers a gift, of course.

Wrong, wrong, wrong. Wedding gifts symbolize friends' and families' joy that a couple has begun a new life together. Gifts should be freely given, not wrung out of guests in a form of social blackmail. The proper attitude for bride and groom is not: "This is what I want, and you'd better give it," but "How wonderful for you to remember us at this special time in our lives."

But . . . and this is the big secret . . . there *are* some tactful ways to give guests guidelines. Most guests, wishing to give couples something they will use and enjoy, anxiously seek advice from the couple, their mothers, and their siblings. That's the time to drop wistful hints.

Offbeat gift registries, such as hardware stores, mail-order catalogs, and home decor shops, are another answer (the names of stores given only if asked, of course). Some guests themselves even dream up delightful and creative gifts, such as concert tickets or museum membership.

And now that the couple has it, what do they do? No matter how dreadful the gift, brides and grooms should always answer promptly with a thank-you note.

GIMME, GIMME, GIMME

One bride wanted to make things easy for her guests — and herself. She didn't want the bother of having to return unwanted or duplicate gifts, so she sent a list of stores where she was registered in her wedding invitations. And if that weren't bad enough, another bride sent guests a list of the gifts she wanted — with their catalog numbers.

HOW DOES A COUPLE AVOID BEING LABELED GREEDY AND MANNERLESS?

◆ Stick to one store, or maybe two if both carry your patterns and are more convenient geographically.

◆ Don't announce where you are registered. What removes the bridal registry from blatant vulgarity is that the guest makes the first move, asking you where you are registered.

◆ Act as if you are overwhelmed that anyone would want to give you a gift. The fiction is that you do not expect gifts but are pleasantly surprised to get them.

TACKY THINGS YOU SHOULD NEVER DO

◈ Announce where you are registered in your newspaper announcements or (worse!) in your wedding invitations.

◈ Tell people what to give you on your wedding invitations.

◈ Put "No gifts" on the invitation.

LETTER FROM A REAL BRIDE: I have agonized over whether "etiquette" will allow me to address the question of wedding gifts in our invitations, such as "If you wish to give a gift, cash would be appreciated. We would like to use the money toward a down payment on a home."—EXPENSIVE PROPOSITION

DEAR EXPENSIVE: Etiquette won't. It is *never* correct to tell anyone what to give you unless you are asked. A gift is something that is given freely, and brides do not have the right to extort household goods, cash, or anything else from their guests.

LETTER FROM A REAL BRIDE: We would like to ask wedding guests to make a donation to charity in lieu of giving us gifts. Harvey wants to enclose notices in the wedding invitations, but I am afraid mentioning gifts in the invitations would be rude. I would prefer to wait until people ask us what we would like and then let them know.—FULL HOUSE

DEAR FULL: What a thoughtful way to share your love with those less fortunate! It's a great idea, but you are right. You should not mention gifts in the invitations, but rather pass along your request by word of mouth.

After their elaborate wedding, one couple realized that they had received nothing from two of the groomsmen. The groom's mother wanted to know how to say something to the guys — tactfully, of course.

THE PLEASURE OF YOUR COMPANY— AND YOUR WALLET

One couple wanted to make sure guests knew exactly how their monetary wedding gifts would be spent. At their reception, the couple set up a wishing well, with a chart marked "Our Honeymoon," "A Night on the Town," and "Our First Home." As their family and friends dropped money into the wishing well, they could indicate — with oh-so-tasteful stick-on hearts — how they wished the couple to use their gift.

LETTER FROM A REAL BRIDE: I have read about engaged couples having a trust account instead of the traditional bridal registry: People deposit money into the account instead of giving them gifts. The money is used for the couple's future, such as a down payment on a house, starting a family, etc. How do you set up such an account? How does one let friends and family know about the account?—MONEY MATTERS

DEAR MONEY: One doesn't. It's more than tacky: It's truly tasteless. One does not invite people to give one money, which is what you are suggesting.

Now, if people *wish* to give you money instead of the traditional china, you may certainly accept it.

If you are worried about a down payment on a house, do what other couples have done: tone down the extravagances of your wedding or honeymoon and use that money for your future home.

LETTER FROM A REAL BRIDE: My fiancé and I plan to marry in January. His mother says being married right after Christmas would cut our gift receipts by one third. I don't doubt that she is right. What should I do?—WORRIED

DEAR WORRIED: Excuse me, but I thought the reason to marry was because two people could not bear to be apart from one another, that they were overjoyed to be spending the rest of their lives together, *not* to see how many presents they could get. I'm so flabbergasted over scheduling weddings at optimum gift-getting times that I don't know what to say to your fiancé's mother, either.

LETTER FROM A REAL BRIDE: When my sister married, she received a number of unneeded gifts because guests did not bother to call to find out about the stores where she was registered. She spent a great deal of time returning the unwanted gifts. I am planning a large wedding, and I don't want the same problem. Is it proper to include a card listing the stores where I am registered in the invitations?—BUSY BRIDE

DEAR BUSY: So you don't have time to take gifts back. Well, put a card like that in your invitations and not only will you not have any gifts to take back, but you also won't have any guests at your wedding, either.

It is *never* proper to ask for gifts, no matter how you try to disguise it as convenience. Your guests took the time and trouble to select, wrap, and deliver gifts they thought you would like. The least you can do is return them with a minimum of complaint about being inconvenienced.

AN ALTERNATIVE TO RETURNING UNWANTED WEDDING GIFTS

"As soon as our wedding appeared in the *Times*, wedding presents poured in. . . . The majority were frightful, and they came in cohorts: fifteen lamps of the same design, forty trays, a hundred and more huge glass vases. . . . When the presents were all arranged, Lady Evelyn looked at them reflectively.

"The glass will be the easiest," she said. "It only needs a good kick."

She said silver was more of a problem. "Walter and I had such luck. *All* of ours was stolen

RECYCLED GIFTS

Oops! One newlywed couple, on a tight budget but blessed with an abundance of wedding gifts, decided to recycle a gift still in its box when invited to the wedding of friends. They were horrified to learn from their mystified friends that the box contained a card from the original giver.

The moral of this story: There's nothing wrong with recycling unneeded wedding presents, but always look in the package first.

THOSE PESKY THANK-YOU NOTES

What's the tackiest thing a couple could ever do? Not thanking people for wedding presents—in writing. There is no excuse. Not only have your guests cared enough about you to spend money on you, they also made sure the gift was wrapped and delivered. They tried hard to please you.

A proper thank-you note takes perhaps six minutes to write. These tacky trends are not acceptable substitutes:

♥ Janice was appalled when she received a pre-printed thank-you note from a couple. The note said, "We appreciate your attending our wedding. Thank you very much for the _____."

♥ One bride was even worse. She had generic thank-you notes printed up that said: "Thank you so much for your kind and thoughtful gift. We enjoyed having you at our wedding." Sure. She really cared.

♥ One couple received a thank-you note from some newlyweds that was addressed: "Dear Friends." Another couple received a note thanking them for the wrong gift. Yet another was thanked verbally by the bride—she happened to bump into them at a party. She never did write them a note.

Guests Can Be Tacky, Too

ooooo

Being a guest at a wedding is an honor and an awesome responsibility. Guests should remember that the bride and groom could have invited anyone in the world to the most important event of their lives, and they asked *you*. They think that much of you, so let's try to live up to that honor, please.

That's where the responsibility comes in. You owe it to them to make sure you don't omit any of your duties as a good guest. Here is a list of guest screwups guaranteed to drive brides crazy:

IGNORING INVITATIONS

Not all social bungles are committed by the wedding party. An alarming number of guests fall prey to this one. RSVPs should be answered in writing the day after an invitation is received. *Never* assume that the bride will just "know" you will be there.

BRINGING UNINVITED GUESTS (AND THIS INCLUDES CHILDREN)

"Uninvited guests" is an oxymoron, because if people aren't invited, they aren't guests. They are party crashers. Only the people whose names are on the invitation are being asked to attend.

No one should assume (or ask) to bring (a) a date; (b) children; or (c) an old friend who's in town. Weddings are expensive, and families often have calculated down to the penny. Don't bring an extra mouth.

LETTER FROM A REAL BRIDE: My fiancé and I are getting married in a small ceremony with just family and close friends. How do we tactfully request that small children of the guests not attend?—ADULTS ONLY

DEAR ADULTS: Don't invite them.

You may wish to drop a hint—politely and in a most regretful manner—to those guests who are quite enamored of their offspring that you are just devastated that you cannot include children at your wedding.

ASKING IF YOU WILL BE INVITED

This puts the bride on the spot and makes her feel bad. She may have a limited budget, and after she includes all of her great-aunts on her mother's side, there is no room for friends.

We're all adults now, and there's a rule we should have learned in kindergarten: Not everyone can be invited. Be grown-up about this, please.

ACCEPTING THE INVITATION AND THEN NOT SHOWING UP

The ultimate faux pas. Only death or a major accident saves you from this one. Don't think the bride and her family won't notice that you're not there in the crowd. They've calculated down to the penny. They'll know. And they'll ask you about it later!

BEING LATE

Unlike most social events, weddings begin promptly on time—unless there's been some calamity, such as a missing groom!

Plan to arrive 15 to 30 minutes ahead of time (more if it will be a big wedding). Otherwise, you may be marching behind the bride as she comes down the aisle.

STIFFING THE COUPLE—NO GIFT

An invitation to a wedding requires that a gift be sent. Some etiquette guides say you need only send one if you attend the wedding, but that looks too much like a gift is the price of admission.

Besides, you want to show the bride and groom how happy you are as they start a life together.

WEARING THE "WRONG" COLOR

Some brides get in a snit if guests show up wearing the same color as the bridesmaids. If this happens to you, forget it. It's not your problem. How could you know what color the bridesmaids are wearing before the wedding— unless you are a so-called "friend" who is mad because she didn't get asked to be a bridesmaid.

MAKING SNIDE REMARKS ABOUT THE WEDDING

Weddings have a built-in titter factor. After all, it *is* hard not to laugh when the bridesmaids arrive in electric blue lace Madonna gloves.

But let's be charitable. Hold those guffaws—at least until you get home.

REARRANGING THE PLACE CARDS

Many thoughtful brides and grooms go to great trouble to make their seating arrangements. They want members of their families to get to know one another and try to seat their friends with people who have similar interests.

People who sit in the wrong place—or worse yet, rearrange the place cards—throw everything off. It's a domino effect: The guest whose place is occupied has to find somewhere else to sit, and soon no one is where he or she is meant to be.

Again, we're all adults here. Sit where you are supposed to sit. You only have to endure it for three hours at the most. Besides, you might make new friends and have a wonderful time in spite of yourself.

INSISTING ON SINGING AT THE RECEPTION

The bandleader or the deejay has a carefully chosen list of songs that have been organized to control the flow of the party. Don't disrupt things by grabbing a microphone and insisting on singing.

You know who you are if you are guilty of this faux pas. What you obviously don't know is that you can't sing.

WALKING OFF WITH THE CENTERPIECES

Some brides and grooms provide guests with little mementos of the wedding, but the centerpieces aren't favors. Don't walk off with the decorations unless instructed to, please.

PUSHING YOUR WAY INTO THE PHOTOS
and/or Directing the Photographer to Shoot Your Family

The photographer has a job to do, and it's not to take photos of you and yours. The bride and groom have arranged for the photographer to shoot certain people at the wedding. He or she may be working on an hourly plan, so all of the time is allotted. Stay out of the way. After all, you don't want the bride and groom to open their proofs and see only photos of you.

FIGHTING OVER THE BRIDE'S BOUQUET

Catching the bouquet is a tradition that has come to mean that you will be the next to marry, but it's not worth risking a broken arm for. Besides, do you really want people to think you are that desperate?

A 10-year-old girl caught the bouquet at a New Jersey wedding. Her furious mother stalked out of the crowd, took the flowers away from the child, and tossed them back to the bride.

IGNORING THE OTHER GUESTS

Being a guest is an honor that comes with the responsibility of socializing with other guests. People give parties because they want their friends to get to know each other. The same goes for weddings. The happy couple wants the people they love to become friends, too. So, don't sit in a corner. Circulate!

FIGHTING AT THE RECEPTION AND/OR GETTING DRUNK

These taboos also fall under the category of guest responsibilities. Fighting and getting drunk not only upset the bride, but they are pretty embarrassing when you remember them the next day.

SMOKING

Smokers feel unwanted and unloved these days, but their habit, no matter how they try to control the smoke, intrudes on other people. A smoker once argued with me that a true host would let smokers light up because he should do anything for his guests' comfort. I think that is taking hospitality too far. Besides, smoking bothers the other guests.

Don't make brides resort to those tacky little "no smoking" signs on each table at the reception. Just assume that you can't. A dearth of ashtrays is a good clue.

OVERHEARD OVER THE BAND AT A WEDDING: "This is the first wedding reception I've ever been to without a disc jockey."

WHAT TO WEAR

♥ DO dress in the spirit of the occasion: a festive dress with elegant accents. And nothing dresses up a daytime outfit like a hat.

♥ DON'T try to upstage the bride.

♥ DON'T wear work clothes. A wedding is no place for a serious suit.

♥ DON'T wear black leather that looks as if it belongs on a motorcycle.

♥ DON'T pull out an old bridesmaid dress. You'll look like you're wearing . . . an old bridesmaid dress.

QUICK CHANGE ARTISTS

The father of the bride was startled when he walked out into the parking lot of the country club and found a couple in their underwear. Friends of his daughter's, they were changing clothes before leaving for another party.

REPONDEZ, S'IL VOUS PLAÎT

"When I sent out my wedding invitations," says Emily, "I refused to have those tacky response cards. I was sure my friends would know the proper way to respond, with a nicely written note. And I was right. People wrote lovely notes that I will treasure always, but I couldn't believe it when I heard that some guests thought I was tacky—because I omitted response cards!"

Some people have become so accustomed to response cards that they think the BRIDE is tacky if she doesn't send the pesky little things.

So the question is: Do we pander to other people's lack of manners by making things so easy for them that all they have to do is fill in the blanks? Well, you know your friends.

NO WHINING

Weddings aren't supposed to be a party where you (a) get drunk, (b) meet someone, or (c) order what you want for dinner. The purpose is to get two people who love each other married in front of joyous friends and family. Everything else is just icing on the wedding cake, so to speak.

The bride and groom want their guests to have

a good time, but remember that you are being entertained as if you were a guest in their home. You must accept their hospitality as it is offered.

TACKIEST WEDDING FAVOR

A plastic keychain with a photo of the bride and groom.

~

Showering the newlywed couple with rice is an ancient custom to ensure fertility. Guests receive little bags of rice (or birdseed at more environmentally correct receptions) that the bridesmaids spent hours filling. Guests are supposed to *open* the bags before tossing, but folks at one Mississippi wedding skipped the intermediate step and threw the bags at the couple. The bride went on her honeymoon with a black eye.

HELL HATH NO FURY...

The wedding was one of the most elegant Atlanta had ever seen, and the reception for 300 guests was held in the city's most elite private club, the Piedmont Driving Club. But when the couple received their wedding photographs, they found that the groom's ex-girlfriend had sneaked into the reception and was in almost every picture.

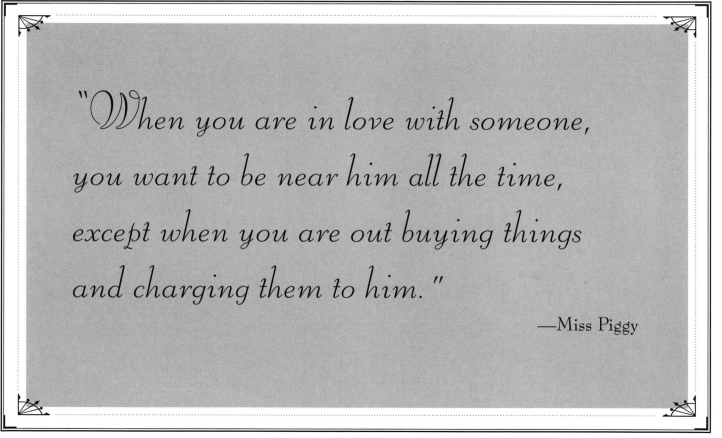

"When you are in love with someone,
you want to be near him all the time,
except when you are out buying things
and charging them to him."

—Miss Piggy

5

The Tackiest Brides in the World

The Brides' Tacky Hall of Shame is reserved for brides on their way to committing Sins of Tackiness. But I don't think they are beyond redemption. Here are their letters and my advice to them:

~

Q. My fiancé and I have begun discussing whom we want in the wedding party. One of my close friends has asked me if she can be the maid of honor. I didn't answer her, but the truth is—I don't even want her to be a bridesmaid. She and my fiancé do not like each other, but the real reason is her appearance. She weighs approximately 350 pounds. I would never want to hurt her, but I want my wedding to be "perfect" or as close as it can be. I could ask her to serve or attend the guest book, but she would be offended. She is truly my friend, but I don't want my wedding to be ridiculed.
— NO FATTIES

DEAR NO: If she were truly your friend, you would not consider your "perfect wedding ridiculed" because of her 350 pounds. Life isn't perfect, and you will find that family and friends will never fit in the neat little design you have planned for them.

You don't want advice on etiquette. You want approval to leave your friend out because she is fat. Well, good manners are the courteous way of treating everyone, no matter what her dress size.

~

Q. My fiancé and I can't decide on colors. He would like to wear metallic blue, and I would like him to wear red or pink. Would there be anything wrong with letting the ushers and the best man wear all the same colors and letting the bridesmaids and maid of honor wear their partners' color?

— PEACOCK

DEAR PEACOCK: Just a minute. I am temporarily blinded by the glare from that metallic blue thought. We aren't talking tuxedos here, are we?

No, of course not. Ties and cummerbunds. Well, that's better, but not much. The trend lately has been toward evening wear with touches of color for the males of our species, and I confess that red, and sometimes pink, bow ties and cummerbunds do pop up at festive times of the year, such as Christmas.

But consider this: Years from now, when you look at your wedding pictures, are you going to want to see the members of your wed-

ding dressed in something classic that never goes out of style? Or will you see dated outfits that remind you of your dreadful eleventh-grade prom photos?

Black is never wrong, and it goes with any color you choose for your bridesmaids' dresses.

～

Q. I am planning to have a wedding vow renewal. I was married four years ago. The wedding was very nice, but I had a matron of honor who was very mean and cruel. She talked behind my back about me. She said that I messed up her brother's wedding, which was not true. She left a great sadness in my heart. Even on my honeymoon, I thought about her. She hurt me purposely. The director of my wedding was also a complete disaster. Prior to the rehearsal, she had not seen the church, etc. My husband did not know where to stand.

Do you have any information and suggestions concerning vow renewals? I want to redo the occasion and erase the sad, hurting memories. This time it will be total bliss. My color scheme will be different this time, but everything else will be the same.

— TWO-TIME BRIDE

DEAR TWO-TIME: Sorry, dear. What you really are after is another wedding, not a service to reaffirm your vows. Those are quiet, religious services usually celebrated at a major anniversary. There are no bridesmaids, much less color schemes.

My advice is to go on with your life. Stop reading bride magazines and dwelling on past slights. If you want to have a big celebration, have an anniversary party—and don't invite anyone who's ever been mean to you.

Q. Is it proper to invite my psychiatrist and my psychologist to my wedding? They helped me to get to this happy point in my life, and I would like them to be a part of it.

— DOCTOR'S ORDERS

DEAR ORDERS: You may invite whomever you wish to your wedding. It is preferable that wedding guests have some sort of relationship to the bride or the groom other than simply knowing their names, and a psychiatrist and a psychologist certainly would meet those requirements. You must promise, however, not to be depressed if they are unable to attend.

❧

Q. I am being married for the second time to the same man. Is it all right to wear a white wedding dress? (It would not be the same one I wore the first time!)   — DOUBLE YOUR PLEASURE

DEAR DOUBLE: We're glad you two have kissed and made up. Second weddings to the first spouse are a growing trend. Sometimes separation helps the heart grow fonder, giving couples a chance to reflect on the relationship without the stress of trying to make it work. They realize that hey! my spouse wasn't so bad after all. Those qualities you loved the first time are still there, and you are willing to negotiate the rest.

Treat this wedding like you would any other second marriage. A smaller marriage ceremony—to which friends are invited by telephone or letter instead of formal invitations—although you could have a blow-out reception to celebrate.

If you wear white, expect some criticism. Why not select something you can wear again, doubling your pleasure in your wardrobe, too.

By the way, when counting up your wedding anniversaries, there is no need to start over at one. Simply total the number of years you have been together, ignoring the number of years you were divorced.

～

Q. This is my second marriage and his first. I want to have a medium-sized wedding with the works—white gown, groomsmen, bridesmaids, etc. Is it still the tradition that the bride's parents pay for the wedding or do we?

— TEXAS TWO-STEP

DEAR TEXAS: Once, wearing white as a second-time bride was scandalous. White was considered a sign of virginity.

Unfortunately, improprieties become accepted with use, and wearing white the second time around is no longer taboo (although we think three times is pushing it). We etiquette mavens have skirted the issue by declaring white acceptable for the "pure in heart."

A wedding is supposed to be a joyous occasion as couples celebrate a new life together. It is a day that should not be tainted by past mistakes. So if you want to wear white, go ahead. But be warned that there are still those who talk, but I hope they are not on your guest list.

I do think that a second-time bride should tone down the festivities. Dozens of bridesmaids and an army of groomsmen is too much. Please limit the size of your wedding party.

As for who pays for the gala, of course it's your turn. Your parents have already done their share.

~

Q. What is the proper etiquette for a maid of honor to drop out of a wedding party? My maid of honor backed out six months before my wedding. I found an old etiquette book that says the only acceptable excuse is a death in her family. Also, since she backed out a month before the shower, she requested her deposit back. Is this proper? Should I have returned her deposit?

— MAID OF DISHONOR

DEAR MAID: In the past, the only acceptable excuses were illness or a death. Now I would like to add another category: careers. With more women in high-powered jobs, there may be instances when doing a deal takes precedence. But let's not abuse this, please.

As for returning the money, I would. Not only is it the gracious thing to do, but it would also get her out of your hair. But I must confess: I've never come across a bride who took deposits from her bridesmaids to ensure their attendance at a shower. Showers are parties thrown by friends, not the bride or her family. Perhaps your friend had reason for wanting out.

~

Q. My daughter is having a small family wedding in December, followed by a large reception in a big private home. Our problem is that our guest list seems to have a life of its own: It keeps growing! We are concerned that the house will not be able to accommodate the number of guests. I would like to know if we could invite guests for two different times. The early group would be older people who don't go out at night, and the later group would be younger friends. Is this acceptable? We don't want to cut our list and hurt feelings.
— TOO MANY FRIENDS

DEAR TOO MANY: And just what are these young people to do in the time between the wedding and the reception? A wedding is not like a factory, with two shifts. Cut your guest list or move your reception.

One alternative is adding a tent on the lawn (you can put the band out there). This way you can have your wedding cake and eat it, too.

~

Q. I have been married for three years. We had a very small ceremony in which my mother and my mother-in-law took total charge. For our fifth anniversary, we would like to renew our vows in a traditional wedding ceremony. Would this be out of the question?
— ONCE IS NOT ENOUGH

DEAR ONCE: A renewal of vows is a religious ceremony made meaningful after twenty or thirty years of marriage. It is *not* a chance to wear a long gown and have bridesmaids. Having a blow-out anniversary party instead may satisfy your craving for a festive celebration of your own.

~

Q. My son is getting married and we are hosting a casual dinner for about 65 people. We want to include children of out-of-state guests and dates for the groomsmen and bridesmaids. I had planned to order the invitations with an inner envelope for adding children's names or "and guest" (for the attendants' dates). But the salesclerk at a large Birmingham engraving company told me this was not acceptable and in poor taste. She said the attendants will know to invite a guest and the families will automatically bring their children. What's correct?

— MOTHER OF THE GROOM

DEAR MOTHER: No wonder children keep showing up where they're not wanted, with "wedding advisors" like that one around!

People with manners know that invitations are meant only for the people whose names are on the envelope. That clerk is doing a disservice.

Your problem is easy to solve. You are correct about not listing the parents' and the children's names on the outer envelope. Instead, send small children their own invitations. Think how excited they will be. Their names should be written:

The Misses Brown

The Messrs. Brown (brothers' names below sisters)

Children over eighteen should, of course, receive their own invitations.

As for the attendants' dates, "guest of" is a phrase that should *never* be used. Get the names and addresses and send these guests their own invitations.

~

Q. My fiancé is of another race. My family loves him, but many of my friends don't know him. Should I tell my friends that he is a different race? Should I enclose personal notes with the invitations telling them about him?
— BRIDAL EQUALITY

DEAR EQUAL: Why do you feel like your friends need to know your fiancé's race beforehand? Are you afraid they will walk out of the church? If he were of the same race as you, would you notify them of that?

I think you see how silly your question is. All that counts is that you and your family love and accept your fiancé, but perhaps you have some doubts you are not admitting to yourself.

Perhaps you should look further into those doubts with counseling before promising "till death do us part."

If you have any concerns about friends who might not accept your fiancé, perhaps their names should be omitted from your guest list.

~

Q. My father and my mother do not get along. He wants to come to the wedding, but I know there is going to be a fight. He has promised not to speak to her. Should I let him come?

— HURT AND WORRIED

DEAR HURT: Your parents are adults and should behave as such, at least long enough to get you married off. Your father has promised his cooperation, so tell your mother how you feel and ask for her help, too. Then, all you can do is trust them—but I wouldn't leave them alone together.

~

Q. Recently I have been experiencing the wedding "blahs" trying to please only me, yet also being ruled and run down by everyone else. Because of expenses—dinner is $30 a person—I am not able to afford to invite escorts for my single women friends. One of my friends of twenty years decided that if she couldn't bring a date, she doesn't need to spend money on a dress. Her attitude is: "My dress cost will be equal to the $60 you would spend on me and an escort." She dropped out of the wedding party. Was I wrong in not letting her invite a guest? She doesn't have a boyfriend, so she would have to go out and find someone just to say "Look who my date is."

— WEDDING BELLE BLUES

DEAR BLUES: No, it was your friend's choice not to be in your wedding. A wedding is not a singles mixer, and singles should not expect to be able to bring their latest love interests, especially if the bride and groom do not know them.

~

Q. My mother refuses to come to the wedding if there is any alcohol whatsoever. We are willing to oblige her, but my question is: should we make a note on our invitations that no alcohol will be served?

— NO BARMAID

DEAR NO: Why? You are inviting people to a wedding, not a cocktail party. The religious ceremony, not the reception, is the most important part of the day. Guests who care about you will not base their acceptances upon what you are serving at the reception. They are delighted to accept your gracious hospitality, no matter whether it takes the form of Dom Perignon or Kool-Aid.

❦

Q. I am being criticized because I chose to have all the gentlemen in formal black tie and tuxedos. My ceremony will be at 3:30 on a Saturday afternoon. Our reception begins at 7:00 p.m., with a cocktail hour from 6:00 to 7:00. The criticism is that the timing makes the wedding informal, not formal. I've always dreamed of a beautiful affair with men in tuxedos and women in long gowns and beautiful jewelry. Is my timing "socially unacceptable"? If I do make it formal, where should I state it: at the bottom of the invitation or on the reception card?

— TIME OUT

DEAR TIME: What you have created is a beast with two heads: a formal daytime wedding and a formal evening reception. Dress is not the same for both.

Dress for a formal daytime wedding is less elegant than for an evening one. Tuxedos should not be worn at weddings before 6:00, nor would female guests wear long gowns with lots of jewelry.

If you want men to wear tuxedos, you state "Black Tie" in the lower right-hand corner of your invitation. Otherwise, you are going to have men showing up in dark suits and women in nice dresses with simple jewelry, the proper attire for a wedding at 3:30 in the afternoon.

❦

Q. We asked a family member to be a groomsman after he had already planned to attend the wedding. Do we have to give him a gift?

— TIGHT-FISTED BRIDE

DEAR TIGHT: Each person in the wedding party should receive a gift, no matter what. Stiffing someone is not the gracious thing to do.

~

Q. Is it bad etiquette to request a "money tree" on our wedding invitation or response card? We certainly do not mean to offend anyone, but we do not need china, silver, or toasters.

— GREEDY BRIDE NO. 1

DEAR GREEDY BRIDE NO. 1: Why don't you just print an admission price on the wedding invitation and sell tickets at the door? That's basically what you are suggesting.

We all know that gifts are part of getting married, but the delightful pretense is that gifts are a happy by-product of weddings. Your friends want to show you their good wishes by commemorating the day. You as a bride must go along with that, or be thought crass and crude.

On the other hand, thoughtful friends and family—the people who know and love you, the only people who should be invited to your wedding—will know that you don't need toasters. They will ask you what you need. *Then* you can tell them.

~

Q. My fiancé and I are well established and have been living together. Is it appropriate to have a wishing well at the reception for gifts of cash and checks?

— GREEDY BRIDE NO. 2

DEAR GREEDY BRIDE NO. 2: Not by me. It's too blatant a grab for gifts.

In the South, gifts of money are sent before the wedding, but in some parts of the country and among some ethnic groups, cash is pressed discreetly upon the bride during dances at the reception. She carries a silk handbag or wears an apron with large pockets for the monetary gifts. In some countries, it is customary to pin money on the bride. But please, no wishing wells.

~

Q. My fiancé and I are in our early thirties. Since he has been married before and I have a love for beautiful belongings, we have everything we need materially. Needless to say, I will not be registering. However, cash is always welcome. How does one request this, if one should?

— GREEDY BRIDE NO. 3

DEAR GREEDY BRIDE NO. 3: One shouldn't.

Q. My reception will be an elegant black-tie affair. Is it tacky to print "Adult Reception" on the invitations? Many of my cousins have small children and do not know what proper etiquette entails.

— NO KIDS, PLEASE

DEAR NO KIDS: A proper invitation would *never* say "Adult Reception." That sounds like a movie ratings code. And don't pack your invitations with notes about how you would love to include the children, but you just can't. If you tell people you can't afford for them to bring the kids, they will offer to pay for the little darlings.

Instead, the correct bride addresses invitations

to the people she is inviting to her reception. She handles relatives who might not realize that invitations addressed only to "Mr. and Mrs. Local Yokel" are meant only for themselves and not their offspring by calling the couple to make sure they understand.

In the course of conversation, she might say, "Oh, I wish we could have little Suzy and the other children, but this is an adult party and won't we have fun!" She may enlist her mother and future mother-in-law to help with this task.

As a final precaution, the smart bride has a nursery, where youngsters may be deposited.

~

Q. We are having a large wedding with a sit-down dinner. With everything else we are planning, we can't afford an open bar. Is it proper to have a cash bar at a wedding reception?
— CHEERS

DEAR CHEERS: It is *never* proper to ask guests to pay for their own refreshments. It is horribly rude to have a cash bar at a wedding reception. Friends and family are invited to a wedding because the couple wants them to share in their joy. If the couple cannot afford to offer mixed drinks, they should switch to less expensive beverages or cut back in another area.

~

Q. My fiancé wants to play a trick at our wedding reception. Instead of pulling off my garter, he intends to produce a pair of panties.
—WHATTA GUY!

DEAR WHATTA: This ranks right up there with his stuffing the cake into your mouth. If you wish to be embarrassed, go along with his plans. But I'd think twice about marrying a man whose idea of fun is ridiculing his wife.

Q. My husband and I eloped five years ago. Now we are ready to have our wedding with "all the trimmings." Is it considered bad taste to have a wedding on a day other than the day you were originally married? What kind of invitation should we give people who know we are already married? It has been my dream to wear a stark white wedding dress (besides, I look dreadful in pastels). Is it improper to wear white and a veil if you are not a virgin? Is it awkward to have your father give you away after you have been married for five years? Should we register for gifts? Do you think bachelor and bachelorette parties are out of the question?

— WANTS IT ALL

DEAR WANTS: Face it. You are married. You can't go back. If you want to have a big

party and wear a white dress, do it, but don't try to call it a wedding. Five years is too long to wait to have a wedding "with all trimmings" after a civil ceremony. You are making a mockery of the commitment and love represented by a wedding.

What you want is to be queen for the day,

and what you are planning is in such poor taste that I have no advice other than "don't."

~

Q. My mother and I disagree over how to address my wedding invitations. I say if I am sending an invitation to a single friend, it should be addressed "and guest." My mother claims it should be only the person's name and that he or she will know it's okay to bring a guest. I have asked many of my single friends, and they said if the invitation didn't read "and guest," they wouldn't bring one. We are planning a formal wedding and want to be "correct." Who's right?

— MISS PERFECT

DEAR MISS: Neither of you. Invitations should never be addressed to "and guest." If you wish one of your friends to bring an escort to your wedding, then find out the date's name and send him or her an invitation. That is the only proper way to invite people to your wedding. "And guest" is improper and is not done.

As for guests to assume that they may bring an escort—that's even worse. An invitation is meant only for the person whose name is on the envelope.

DON'T EXPECT ANOTHER WEDDING PRESENT FROM US

Linda Lou Essex of Anderson, Indiana, has had 21 monogamous weddings to 15 different men. Glyn "Scotty" De Moss Wolff of Blythe, California, a former Baptist minister, has married 27 wives one at a time.   —*The Guinness Book of World Records*

~

TACKY, TACKY, TACKY

Real estate magnate Donald Trump and his former wife, Ivana, had a "carnal contract," by which, it seems, Ivana accepted that adultery was part of their American marriage—so long as both partners could indulge in it. —*The Guinness Book of Marriage*

~

Q. We are planning a formal sit-down dinner and would like to offer two entrées so guests will have a choice. Since the chefs need to know ahead of time how much of each to prepare, is it appropriate to ask somewhere on the invitation? Or could guests indicate their preference on the response cards?

—ACCOMMODATING COUPLE

DEAR ACCOMMODATING: Are you having a wedding or running a restaurant? It would be extremely tacky to have spaces to check roast beef or chicken on the response card.

Instead, have the caterer serve small portions of each entrée artfully arranged on the same plate. Talk to your caterer about this.

~

Q. I cannot find the answer to our problem in any etiquette books. We are planning a small wedding of approximately seventy-five people with a limited budget. Our reception will be a cocktail hour with an open bar followed by a sit-down dinner and dancing. During the remainder of the reception (about three hours), it will be cash bar. Do we print this news on the reception card, enclose a handwritten note, or let people know by word of mouth?

— PLEASE PAY UP

DEAR PLEASE: The reason you can't find the answer to the question of a cash bar in any etiquette books is because no etiquette consultant could conceive of anything so tasteless as inviting people to a wedding reception with a cash bar. You have invited your friends and your family as your guests. It is horrible manners to charge them to come to your party.

If your budget will not accommodate the dinner *and* drinks for your guests, then you need to scale down your reception. Have a cocktail party with heavy hors d'oeuvres or cancel the dancing.

~

Q. I need to get an exact head count for my reception. I thought I could enclose a card in my invitations asking, "Number attending _____." Our wedding will be in New York, and I want to give our guests the option of bringing someone since they will be traveling. I also want to give unmarried guests the chance to bring a date without my having to ask for names and addresses. If you are single and not involved with anyone, you should not bring an escort, but that is a decision I would rather leave to my guests.

— COUNTING NOSES

DEAR COUNTING: Sorry, but I disagree. You are making up your own etiquette as you go along instead of abiding by decades-old guidelines that everyone knows and understands. How are your guests supposed to "know" who's allowed to bring an escort and who's not? Osmosis? The Vulcan mind-meld?

If you want people to feel free to come to your wedding with an escort, call them and ask them for names and addresses. Then *invite* those people, too. It is more work for you, but otherwise you are insulting your guests. You are seeing them as a number and not even bothering to learn their names.

~

Q. I am marrying for the first time, but this will be my fiancé's second marriage. I know that it is inappropriate for a second-time bride to wear white, but does the same rule go for the groom? Would it be best to wear white or ivory?

— GENDER BENDER

DEAR GENDER: I don't like white tuxedos. Somehow the groom always tends to look like an ice cream cone . . . oh, for you? The white rule applies only to the bride. It's the idea of innocence and purity. Choose whichever looks best on you.

Help stamp out tackiness! We want to hear about your experiences with tacky brides and other boors. Please send your stories to

Martha Woodham
c/o Longstreet Press
2140 Newmarket Parkway
Suite 118
Marietta, GA 30067

Index

ATTENDANTS
Bridesmaids, 1, 3, 5, 6
Flower girls, 5, 62-63
Groomsmen, 1, 3
Maid of honor, 6
Matron of honor, 4, 6
Ringbearer, 63
Whom to ask, 1, 5, 115

ATTIRE
Black-tie, 14, 24, 116, 124
Brides, 17, 24
Bridesmaids, 11-12
Garters, 24
Gloves, 17

Grooms, 13, 16
Guests, 13, 16
Mothers, 9-11
Rules, 15
Second-time brides, 9, 117
Veils, 24
Wearing white, 9, 16, 118

THE BRIDE
Engagement, 12
Garters, 24
Selfish, 21
Veils, 25
Who gives away, 2

BRIDESMAIDS
Attire, 72
And the groom, 71
What to do and not to do, 70-71,
    119-20, 123
Whining, 70
Whom to ask, 1, 72

CEREMONY
Great ideas, 57-58
Mixed marriages, 58
Music, 55-56
Theme weddings, 48-52
Wedding programs, 24, 55

CHILDREN
    Invited or invited? 61-62
    In the wedding party, 57, 62, 63
    Second weddings, 58

FAMILY
    Deceased parents, 26, 39
    Divorced parents, 21, 65, 69, 122-23
    Fathers, 2, 3, 4, 64-66, 123
    Mothers, 2, 3, 4, 64-66, 70, 123, 124
    Siblings, 1
    Stepmothers, 66-68

GIFTS
    Asking for, 33, 97, 99-101, 125-26
    Displaying gifts, 33
    Invitations, 99-100
    Recycled, 103

    Registering for, 97-98
    Returning, 102
    Sending, 7
    Thank-you notes, 7, 23, 103-4

GUESTS
    Answering invitations, 104, 106
    Attire, 110
    Boorish behavior, 106-9
    Bringing the kids, 78, 85, 105
    Gifts, 104, 106
    Smoking, 110
    The guest list, 40, 43, 117
    Whining, 107, 111

INVITATIONS
    "Adults only" reception, 38, 61-62, 78, 85, 126-27
    Answering, 7

    Budget tips, 42
    Computer help, 40-42
    Deceased parents, 39
    Guests bringing guests, 121-22, 129, 131-32
    Office colleagues, 40
    Parents' names, 35-36, 39
    RSVPs, 7, 38
    Response cards, 40-41
    The guest list, 43
    The "mature" bride's, 37
    Wedding announcements, 44
    Wording, 34-35, 43-44, 124, 129-32

MONEY
    Who pays for the wedding? 7-8, 21, 33, 86-89, 91, 118-19, 130-31
    And wording the invitations, 86

Budget ideas, 83-84, 87
Wretched excess, 92

PUBLICITY
Engagement photos, 33
Newspaper announcements, 30

PHOTOGRAPHY
Photographs, 24
Videotaping, 47

RECEPTIONS
Budget mistakes, 83
Cake knowhow, 83, 85, 89
Children, 78, 81, 85
Drinking, 79, 123-24, 127, 130-31
Menu, 77-78, 91, 127
No smoking, 81-82
Opening gifts, 81

Practical jokes, 79-80, 127
Receiving lines, 79
Timing, 79, 120

REHEARSAL DINNERS, 92

RENEWING YOUR VOWS
Vow-renewal ceremonies, 72-75,
116-17, 120-21, 128-29

SECOND WEDDINGS
Attendants, 59
Children, 59
How big, 58-59
Second-time brides, 9
Showers, 93
Veils, 24
Wearing whites, 9, 16, 132

SHOWERS
Gifts, 93-94
Hosting, 93-94
Second marriages, 93
Whom to invite, 93

THANK-YOU NOTES
Timetable, 1, 7

WEDDING THEMES
Fun and offbeat, 49-52
Tacky, 53-55